Contents

The True Story of
The Monkees

by Andrew Sandov

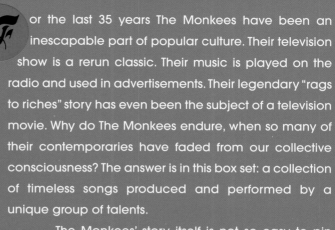

or the last 35 years The Monkees have been an inescapable part of popular culture. Their television show is a rerun classic. Their music is played on the radio and used in advertisements. Their legendary "rags to riches" story has even been the subject of a television movie. Why do The Monkees endure, when so many of their contemporaries have faded from our collective consciousness? The answer is in this box set: a collection of timeless songs produced and performed by a unique group of talents.

The Monkees' story itself is not so easy to pin down. The project was the creation of two "New Hollywood" producers, Bob Rafelson and Bert Schneider. Rafelson was a drifting intellectual, who claimed to have hosted a radio show, written for a Japanese newspaper, and traveled with a band through Mexico before The Monkees story line came to him. "I got the idea for the series in 1962, before Dick Lester's *A Hard Day's Night*," Rafelson explained to Alan Smith in 1967. He also cited his own work in advertising—"a lot of the technique I picked up there." Nevertheless, Rafelson's "technique" meant little to Hollywood executives until Lester's film with The Beatles was a success. "I had a hard time selling it until The Beatles came along," Rafelson later told Monkees biographer Eric Lefcowitz. "The Beatles made it all happen, that's the reality," agreed Bert Schneider, who helped Rafelson sell the premise of an out-of-work rock band to his father, Columbia Pictures president Abe Schneider. On April 16, 1965, Screen Gems, the television division of Columbia Pictures, bought the Rafelson and Schneider concept, giving the go-ahead to cast and shoot a pilot.

In early September 1965 the two producers, under the banner of Raybert Productions, placed ads in *Variety* and *The Hollywood Reporter* seeking "folk & roll musicians." The open cattle call drew as many as 400 applicants—a sundry group of musicians, actors, and Los Angeles scenesters. "When we started to do interviews for prospective Monkees, we were literally seeing people hour by hour," Rafelson remembered. "It was a lot of fun, and we used to do nutty things to see what

sort of reaction we got from the applicants. We ended up having musical jam sessions in the office." By October they'd weeded through the mass of hipsters and hopefuls, selecting the final four.

Twenty-year-old Micky Dolenz was a former child actor best known for his starring role in the late-'50s television series *Circus Boy*. As a teenager, Dolenz sang folk music with his sister Coco, later turning to rock 'n' roll with such ad hoc outfits as The Missing Links and Micky & The One Nighters. Though Dolenz was still getting sporadic acting work in 1965, he was covering his bases by taking a drafting course at the local city college.

Davy Jones was a 20-year-old amateur jockey-turned-Broadway musical actor. Picking up roles at an early age in BBC radio plays and the British television institution *Coronation Street*, Jones had actually gained the most recognition for his turn as the Artful Dodger in the stage version of *Oliver!* A later stage part as Sam Weller in *Pickwick* brought Davy to Los Angeles, where he cut a number of sides for Columbia Pictures' Colpix record label. One of these tracks, the ultratwee "What Are We Going To Do?" slipped into the bottom of the *Billboard* Pop chart for three weeks in August '65. A slight feat, indeed, but with it came a national fan club, full-page spreads in several teen magazines, and appearances on *Shindig!* and *Where The Action Is*. Jones was under exclusive contract to Columbia Pictures, and the studio was anxious to find a vehicle for their rising star. "Davy is the one I had the most doubts about," Rafelson later confessed. "Davy had less contact with rock 'n' roll than any of the others, and although he had acting experience, I wasn't sure if he would be able to get into the spirit of the thing."

Conversely, Rafelson's last two choices had the genuine "folk & roll" credentials called for in his original ad. "There was one guy, Steve Stills, whom I liked enormously," Rafelson said. "Unfortunately, he wasn't quite right. When he realized he wasn't

going to make it, he suggested I get in touch with someone he knew, Peter Thorkelson. I found him working as a dishwasher—not even a musician. But when I heard him, I was knocked out." Twenty-four-year-old Peter Thorkelson (soon renamed Peter Tork) had made an abortive attempt at a group with Stills called The Buffalo Fish. With Tork now cast in the show, Stills formed a band that became a seminal folk/country-rock outfit, The Buffalo Springfield.

It was The Buffalo Springfield's first manager, Barry Friedman, who suggested that Michael Nesmith audition for a part in the series. At age 23, Nesmith was a transplanted Texan and newlywed father living hand-to-mouth in Hollywood. Undoubtedly a gifted songwriter, during the early '60s Nesmith toured as a folk singer and released one-off singles for the Highness and Omnibus labels. Later, under the auspices of Bob Krasnow, Nesmith adopted the name Michael Blessing and began recording for the

Colpix label. "They came out to my house to do two arrangements," remembered the late, great jazzman Shorty Rogers, who worked on Michael's Colpix sides. "They said they'd come in separate cars, Krasnow and Michael. Each day the phone would ring, and Michael would say, 'I'm tied up, I can't come today, I'll call you tomorrow and come.' Finally, Friday they showed up, and I said, 'What was going on?' Michael said, 'Oh, gee, my wife and I were living in a car, and we didn't have any gas.'

Coincidentally, Michael had left my number with his wife, and while we were having our first get-together the phone rang. He talked to her, and when he hung the phone up he said, 'I got the job with The Monkees!' It was right in my room that he got the message."

With casting complete, the pilot for *The Monkees* was shot around Los Angeles and San Diego in late November 1965. *Monkees* television director James Frawley says the actors were well cast: "Their personalities are pretty much what you see. Michael was intuitively the leader—very smart, very dry in his attitude and sense of humor. Micky was the comic—did a lot of the slapstick. Peter was a quiet, sensitive guy. Davy was the ladies man. Each one of them was one quarter of the perfect man."

Personality could only take the four so far; now they needed music. Songwriters Tommy Boyce & Bobby Hart were contracted not only to supply the pilot's music but also to conceive a stylistic approach for the mythical group. "The producers didn't give us any lyrical direction or philosophy," Hart says. "We knew that this was going to be the 'American Beatles' visually, and we assumed it made the most sense to do a Beatles-influenced sound—not a rip-off—musically. The pilot show was sold with Tommy and I singing the songs."

Boyce & Hart's music propelled Raybert's visuals to new heights. As a result, NBC, confident about the show's potential for success, purchased it from Screen-Gems/Columbia on January 17, 1966. Moreover, once Raybert grasped how successful *The Monkees* would be with an outstanding and memorable soundtrack, the producers decided a steady flow of high-quality music was mandatory.

"They suddenly realized, 'Well, we got more than we bargained for; we really gotta pay more attention to the music. This is important content,'" says Nesmith. "So they cast about. They asked if I would do some things. I said, 'Well I can do some things, but if I was going to put together a rock 'n' roll band, I don't know that I would put together a band with David, Micky, and Peter. These are good guys to work with, but we all have very different musical tastes.'"

For the next six months Raybert agonized over what to do with the show's music. They really liked the idea of The Monkees themselves actually performing the songs. "I remember having rehearsals before the show started filming," Peter Tork says. "In March or April of '66 we had a rehearsal room and were starting to play together. Ward Sylvester—executive producer on *The Monkees* series—tells me that Capitol Records would have signed us even if we hadn't had a TV show." That notwithstanding, the musical progress was slow. "They did rehearse, but there was a time element involved," remembered the late Lester Sill, who was The Monkees' music coordinator. "They had to get the show on the air, they *had* to prerecord the songs."

The producers realized they needed a large volume of musical material. Don Kirshner, who was the head of Screen Gems Music Publishing, the production entity for The Monkees, was brought in to help. Kirshner, in turn, rounded up his best songwriters and selected about 20 songs to be recorded in Los Angeles by various production teams in June and July.

Nesmith was allowed to produce his own sessions and did his best to include the other Monkees in his work. This was significant because under Kirshner's reign they were strictly forbidden from participating in recordings for anything other than lead-vocal purposes. "I was going to let the boys do their own thing, but my standards were #1

records and hits," Kirshner would later tell Eric Lefcowitz. "In all due respect to Peter Tork, if he came up with a song that was less than a pop hit, I had to say, 'Yea' or 'nay.' I had the creative power to do so."

"One of the things that Don Kirshner did is send a memo that said: 'Absolutely no one is to submit any songs for The Monkees or to play songs to anyone in The Monkees until it's been cleared through me,'" recalls Nesmith. "So Peter said, 'Well, does that mean if I write a song, I can't play it for myself until I play it for you?'"

All this and The Monkees had yet to release a record or be seen outside the confines of an audience-testing booth. As Kirshner explained, he had greater concerns than merely pleasing Nesmith and Tork: "I told people I would outsell The Beatles."

On May 30, 1966, The Beatles released a new single called "Paperback Writer." Bobby Hart remembers hearing it for the first time: "I was pulling into my carport, and I was punching the radio stations, and I heard the tail end—all I heard was the fade-out part. I thought they were saying, 'Take the last train to . . . somethin'." A couple of days later I heard the whole song, and I realized it wasn't about a train or anything. So I said, 'Well since they didn't use it, it's the great start of something else.'" Hart's instincts were rewarded when his "Last Train To Clarksville," The Monkees first single, hit #1 on November 5, 1966.

Kirshner felt both vindicated and empowered by the record's success. He quickly switched into overdrive, creating more product than The Monkees could ever hope to release. Sessions for backing tracks would now be held on the East Coast, where Kirshner lived (he suffered an intense fear of flying), and the finished product would be shipped out to Los Angeles for The Monkees to overdub vocals.

The band members had very little input in the tracks now coming from New York, and Nesmith recalls his reaction upon seeing the finished product: "The first album shows up, and I look at it with horror because it makes it appear as if we are a rock 'n' roll band. There's no credit for the other musicians." After expressing his outrage to the producers, they agreed not to do it again, he says.

Just seven short weeks after "Clarksville" topped the

Photos: Gene Trindl

Photo: Henry Diltz

charts, The Monkees once again held the #1 position on December 31, 1966, with "I'm A Believer." "When Neil Diamond walked in and played it for me, I knew it was a major, major giant song," Kirshner told Eric Lefcowitz. Kirshner's judgment could not be faulted. The record, ultimately The Monkees' biggest hit of all time, charted in more than a dozen countries.

As public demand for The Monkees grew steadily, offers for live concert appearances rolled in. Finally, in December 1966 The Monkees got their first taste of what it was like to be a real band when they mounted a short concert tour. The experience of playing together and doing it themselves changed everything. The four hired hands soon learned that they were not only capable musicians—*they were also quite good*. By early January they were still on the road, gaining confidence with every date. They also picked up something else on the road: *More Of The Monkees*—their second album.

"Don Kirshner came out all proud and all pleased to show us the album," remembers Davy Jones. "Now these songs that were on the album, we were originally told we were recording for the TV show only because they were going to put new songs in every show. After a couple of shows, the company got the idea of putting 'I'm A Believer' or 'Last Train To Clarksville' in this next episode— and every episode for the next six or eight weeks— because it sold records. It wasn't supposed to be that way.

"So when Donnie Kirshner showed up all pleased and said, 'Look, guys, here's your second album,' we all went bloody mad.

Mike Nesmith and Peter Tork especially—'What do you mean, this is *our* album?' They had told us we were going to be doing our own album. That's when it got all funky."

"At which point I quit," says Nesmith. "I made a decision to say, 'I'm not going to sit still for this . . . Bert Schneider and Bob Rafelson instantly got it. They said, 'You know, you're right. What do you think about you guys playing together as a band?'"

Meanwhile, a promise Kirshner had made to Neil Diamond a few months before came back to haunt him. Donnie had vowed that if "I'm A Believer" made #1 he would automatically make a Diamond song the follow-up single. It was when Diamond presented "A Little Bit Me, A Little Bit You" to Kirshner that he sensed his error. This was not a 1 single in his opinion.

Complicating the matter, Jeff Barry, the producer of "I'm A Believer," also wanted payback for his good work, requesting that "She Hangs Out," his own composition, be the flip side. If all that wasn't enough, his "employees," The Monkees, were demanding that a Michael Nesmith song they'd recorded on their own, "The Girl I Knew Somewhere," be released as the next single or various

members would quit. Despite Kirshner's control tactics, he had truly lost his grip on the situation.

Raybert intervened and quietly insisted that Kirshner at least issue "The Girl I Knew Somewhere" as one side of the single in fairness to The Monkees and to save the project from collapsing. "Well, Kirshner set his heels," recalls Nesmith. "He said, 'I'm not gonna do it.' Which ultimately cost Kirshner his job. They fired him." In the aftermath, "A Little Bit Me, A Little Bit You" (with "The Girl I Knew Somewhere" on the flip side) just missed the top of the charts as Kirshner had predicted (it made #2 in April 1967), by which time The Monkees had already completed an album of their own, *Headquarters*.

"*Headquarters* was by far the best album, in the sense that it was us," says Micky Dolenz. "It was honest, it was pure." Musically, the album is impressive in a beautifully naive way. It benefited from sympathetic production by former Turtle Chip Douglas and the skilled engineering of Hank Cicalo. The songs The Monkees contributed may not have been "hits" as such, but they were just as good, if not better than, the tracks Kirshner had selected for *More Of The Monkees.*

"I listen to it now, and it sounds like a pretty good kids' garage album," says Peter Tork, the Monkee to whom *Headquarters* meant the most. "Nobody was a slouch. You don't hear good sophisticated musicians at every post, but that's not the point of a bunch of kids getting together and playing music. The whole point of a band is that you get something that comes out of who's there. That's the difference."

Within two weeks of release, on June 24, 1967, *Headquarters* hit #1. Kirshner was all but a memory for the band who had won their musical independence. Still, they could never surmount the press and public's belief that they were incapable of generating their own music. Nor would they ever be truly forgiven for their past inadequacies. As pop historian Lillian Roxon noted in her definitive 1969 *Rock Encyclopedia*: "Nobody really minded that The Monkees were manufactured entirely in cold blood and for bluntly commercial

reasons. But when, never having played together before, their records hit the top of the charts on the strength of what seemed like nothing more than TV exposure and a good, sound financial push, the bitterness was overwhelming."

Nesmith says that at the very time the press was labeling them as somehow illegitimate and false, he was in fact working to maintain the integrity of the group. "The press went into a full-scale war against us, (saying), 'The Monkees are four guys who have no credits, no credibility whatsoever, who have been trying to trick us into believing that they are a rock band.'"

After Kirshner had been purged and *Headquarters* released, the band decided to change course. Despite the album's commercial success, Nesmith says they wanted to return to the songwriting strategy of their earlier albums, but this time clearly indicating how those songs would come to be.

Stephen Stills with Peter and Davy

The result was *Pisces, Aquarius, Capricorn & Jones Ltd.*, The Monkees' finest album and, truth be told, one of the best records of the '60s. "I thought *Pisces, Aquarius* was the one that caught it all," Nesmith says. "We went back to the basics of making music for the television shows and trying to make good pop records, and I think we did a good job at it."

Nevertheless, the album was a signpost of the group's growing fragmentation. Without the common enemy of Kirshner to unite the members, the group splintered. "They didn't want to have to go through a central interpreter like me," recalls producer Chip Douglas. "Peter kind of drifted away first, and then everybody did. Everyone wanted to do their own songs and produce them the way they wanted to hear them. I was ready to do that Boyce & Hart song 'P.O. Box 9847'—it sort of had that

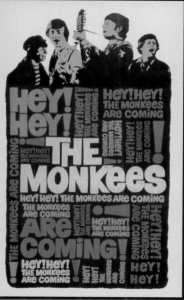

'Paperback Writer' feel on the demo. We passed on it for *Pisces*, and I began to think, 'Well, we should do that one now.' Then somebody said, 'Chip, we're not working with you anymore; we're gonna do our own thing.'"

During late 1967 The Monkees began holding quasi-solo sessions, presaging the *White Album*-era Beatles. "By that time we had all decided that we were going to do our own brand of music—three tracks each on the album," remembers Dolenz. "We got our own songs, our own arrangers and produced our own sessions."

A coterie of friends and admirers sprang up around The Monkees, each of whom decided to work with "their group" on their individual tracks. The outcome was that on any given day during the

making of their next album, *The Birds, The Bees & The Monkees*, each member of the group could be holding a session in up to four different studios around Los Angeles—four times the product at only a fraction of the quality.

The selections on *The Birds, The Bees & The Monkees* were questionable in many respects. Most obviously, the group members had difficulty in selecting their best material; more superior outtakes exist from this album than any of the group's others. Moreover, the lack of group interaction gives a cold feeling to the tracks, especially after the triumphs of *Pisces, Aquarius, Capricorn & Jones Ltd.* and *Headquarters.* Excluding "Daydream

Believer," which was recorded at earlier sessions, Nesmith's "Auntie's Municipal Court" is the only song on the entire album to feature the participation of more than one Monkee. Nevertheless, when released in April '68, *The Birds, The Bees & The Monkees* went gold, peaking at #3 (their first album to miss the top spot).

Emmy Awards banquet, June 5, 1967

Photo: MichaelOchsArchives.com

But the success mattered little to the band, who were by this time embroiled in the production of their first feature film. Work on the film—at first called *Untitled*, later *Changes*, and eventually released as *Head*—and its accompanying soundtrack consumed most of 1968. A lot was riding on this project for the group, who had by now abandoned their television series for dreams of the big screen. However, with the second season of their series still in reruns on NBC and chart records still in quantity, there was no reason the film shouldn't have catapulted The Monkees to even greater heights of fame.

No reason, that is, except that the filmmakers, who also happened to be the creators of The Monkees—Bert Schneider and Bob Rafelson (aided and abetted by an up-and-coming Jack Nicholson)—had

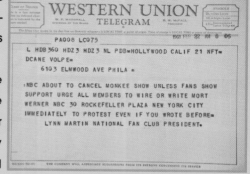

no intention of making a film that would appeal to The Monkees' audience.

"We wanted to do something special," says Peter Tork. "Something a little extraordinary. Something not quite normal. We really didn't want to make another episode of the television show. The four of us, Bert Schneider, Bob, and Jack Nicholson all went to Ojai and talked about what we did and didn't want. We sort of found a common ground. What exactly that was, we wound up leaving to Bob and Jack—the exact script of the movie was basically their idea."

Although over the years *Head* has taken on a cult-classic status, it was a box-office disaster when released in November 1968. Part of the problem was Raybert's subliminally based marketing "Plan A," which made little or no mention of The Monkees. "I think Bert and Bob had given up on The

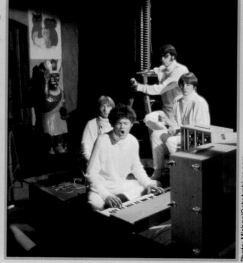

Photo: MichaelOchsArchives.com

Photo: MichaelOchsArchives.com

Monkees at that point," says Tork. "It was their pub-licity decision to have those two-minute commer-cials for *Head* that were so avant-garde as to be positively repulsive. I think that those things were very conscious decisions to deep-six the movie and the entire project. Bert said to me the point was to destroy The Monkees." Charitably, one could say that his point was to get past The Monkees' bubblegum image, but less charitably one could conclude that he wanted to be done with the project, according to Tork.

The accompanying soundtrack to the film, like its parent feature, was an avant-garde release. The packaging—a heavy Mylar sleeve designed to reflect the buyer's own head—bent the presses at RCA's

Photos: Henry Diltz

manufacturing plant and caused the album's release to be delayed by several weeks. The record inside the jacket featured just six songs cut by Jack Nicholson into a collage of dialogue and sounds.

For Tork, *Head* ranks second only to *Headquarters* as his favorite Monkees album: "It's the most diverse and the trippiest. It was really all about trips—going someplace. You know, we used the word in those days very specifically, meaning, not just spacey, but actu-ally involved in some kind of an adventure, as opposed to plodding along, one song after another. *Head*—that was something special. Nicholson coordinated the soundtrack, and he made it different from the movie. It was a differ-ent artistic experience."

In late 1968 The Monkees toured Australia and Japan, turning in their tightest shows ever. "We were playing ('Sunny Girlfriend')

Micky & Samantha Dolenz at the *Head* premiere

in Osaka and the guitar line—the sort of boogie woogie guitar line just up and down the chord—I played on the bass. Basically, we were just a trio for the most part playing live, since Davy didn't play much. But we hit the pocket on that song. We really just locked into something; it was remarkable. Davy came jumping over to me, banging his tambourine. Screaming above the din of the crowd, he said, 'We're going to form a group.' Because it was really good; it was like what you live for as a musician."

Despite this ultimate moment of group unity, the foursome was on its last legs as a unit only weeks later. Their next project was to tape a new television special for NBC. The program, *33 1/3 Revolutions Per Monkee*, was written and produced by Jack Good, a veteran of *Shindig!* and other revolutionary music programs. Nevertheless, the special (completed in mid-December '68) was surprisingly shoddy despite some stellar musical moments.

Nesmith remembers the production as ". . . a little hysterical. I think in the early stages everybody was working together 'cause it was a very interesting idea. In the later stages a lot of people were just coming around because they felt like they could get up next to The Monkees. It was such a huge hit that they thought that they could somehow make their career or fortune on it. So I think this guy Jack Good had some

of that going on. He was supposed to be kind of a quirky and interesting television director. It started to career and get more and more out of control and have less and less to say. He was, I think, in some way trying to grind the same ax that *Head* did so beautifully. He did it clumsily. Sort of the television version of *Head* in a way."

When taping wrapped on the special, Peter Tork announced his intention to leave the band. "I'd always had deep doubts ever since the session for 'Clarksville,'" he recalls. "I walked in there with my guitar, and Tommy Boyce and Bobby Hart looked at me with derision and scorn, like, 'Guitar in your hand, you fool!' I didn't feel like there was any reason for me to be there anymore. I wanted to be in a group."

For Nesmith, Tork's exit meant that he could finally achieve the musical autonomy he'd sought since the group's inception. "I could understand why he wanted to go, 'cause I did too," he says. "But I felt like we hadn't quite finished up. I felt like there was some things that The Monkees were and represented that hadn't been said or done."

Now a trio, The Monkees released their seventh album, *Instant Replay*, in February 1969. Like *The Birds, The Bees & The Monkees*, the record is a musical hodgepodge of tracks recorded at various times with musically disparate units. Although *Instant Replay* reached a respectable #32 on the charts, The Monkees' star wasn't ris-

ing. Acting out of either complete perversity or sheer desperation, Dolenz, Jones, and Nesmith mounted a concert tour with a seven-piece band known as Sam & The Goodtimers. "It was surreal, because Sam & The Goodtimers were a hard-core, black lounge, R&B band, and there they were backing us up," Nesmith remembers.

The Monkees' return to television would be even tougher. Guest shots on variety and talk shows did little to bolster the public's support for the group, who openly fought on screen. In February on *The Glen Campbell Goodtime Hour*, Mike yelled at Davy during a comedy sketch and later in the same segment argued with Micky over whose lines were on the cue card. When the band made a June appearance on Johnny Carson's *Tonight Show* things turned from bad to worse. The Monkees' panel segment featured Micky rambling on about holograms, polygraph testing, and the *TV Guide*. "The Johnny Carson show was pretty strange," admits Dolenz. "I was a big fan, and I got up there and I gave him a hologram. Also I had a copy of something that had been in the *TV Guide* about how to steal a talk show. I started reading that on the air."

An argument between band members after the broadcast placed a further rift into their already strained relations. The end drew nearer when a few days later their concert at the Forest Hills Music Festival was canceled due to low ticket sales. Only two years before they had performed three record-setting concerts at the

same venue; now they couldn't attract enough fans to play one. Morale was at an all-time low when their final long-player as a trio, *The Monkees Present*, was issued in October 1969.

The Monkees Present was originally conceived as a double album of music spotlighting the group members' individual studio efforts. However, by the time this ambitious project reached fruition, Screen Gems scaled back the package. "By that time we were, you know, as cold as yesterday's soup. Nobody would spend any money," Nesmith explains.

As concert audiences dwindled, and recording budgets disappeared, Nesmith saw his future—*without The Monkees.* He left the band in March 1970. "It was just an orderly end to a business deal that had finally come to a close," he says. "I was ready to move. I was a hired writer, a hired actor, and while I had put all of my good-faith creative energies into it, it was not something that grew up around me organically, so I didn't feel like it was the end of anything." Meanwhile, Dolenz and Jones stuck around for their last waltz as a recording act when producer Jeff Barry returned to serve up some funky bubblegum on the album *Changes*.

"By that time it was pretty obvious that the Monkees were over," says Dolenz. "Davy and I were still getting along, but we were mainly ful-

filling a contractual obligation to the record company. At the time, we were all think-ing that we could go on and have our own careers." After some negotiation, Dolenz and Jones were released from their contracts and absolved of any further Monkee responsibilities.

During the early '70s fans saw some interesting and occasionally astounding post-Monkee solo records from Nesmith, Jones, and Dolenz. Ironically, Peter Tork, the first to leave the band and the Monkee most eager for a career centered in music, would remain dormant recordwise until 1981. In 1975 the original foursome recon-

vened to discuss working together again as a group. "We met up at my house in the Hollywood Hills," recalls Dolenz. "I think it was the William Morris Agency who had expressed an interest in putting the act back together. Everybody was very enthusiastic about it on the surface—you know, 'Oh, great, great idea.' But when it got down to the nitty gritty, there were too many con-flicting feelings and attitudes. We only had the one meeting, and I don't think anything else happened after that. There wasn't any animosity. Actually, I remember it being real-ly exciting. Being all together for the first time in quite a few years in the same room. There was a hell of a buzz. Because, we do have—always did and always will—an incredible chemistry between the four of us."

The upshot of the meeting was that, although they couldn't decide on what to do as The Monkees, or even how to do it, they were not totally averse to working together. Jones and Dolenz were espe-cially amenable to teaming up again. By July 1975 they were back on tour with fellow Monkee veterans Tommy Boyce and Bobby Hart. "I think it must have been Tommy o Bobby that put it together," recalls Dolenz. "They knew of an agent who had said, 'I ca get you guys some gigs.' That's when we came up with the 'Guys Who Wrote 'Em and the Guys Who Sang 'Em.' It sounded like a good idea." The foursome's *Great Golde Hits Of The Monkees* tour played amusement parks around the country for a full yea The well-received reunion eventually spun off into an album for Capitol Record (released as *Dolenz, Jones, Boyce & Hart*) and a syndicated television special.

By 1977 Micky and Davy had ventured off on their own. "Davy and I got a job doing a play," says Dolenz. "A musical (version of) *Tom Sawyer*. Then an agent came to us and said, 'Do you and Davy want to go out with a show?' We had to make a decision whether to go out with Tommy and Bobby or just go out by ourselves. I think it was just an economic decision. We could make more money going out just ourselves. We went out and did a couple of summers just as Dolenz and Jones, doing a lot of The Monkees hits and a lot of new material too. After that we went to England to do (Harry Nilsson's musical) *The Point*. That's when Davy and I split up, and I stayed in England."

It wasn't until 1985 that all the group members would consider working together again. The catalyst for this particular reunion was Tork, who, along with concert promoter David Fishof, floated the idea of a 20th anniversary tour the following year. With Dolenz, Jones, Tork, and Nesmith all on board for the event, plans were made, and venues were booked. Concurrently, show cocreator Bert Schneider managed to persuade MTV to run the original *Monkees* series as a marathon, setting off an unexpected resurgence in popularity. All parties were rewarded for their efforts when a brand-new single featuring Dolenz and Tork, "That Was Then, This Is Now," reached the Top 20, and seven different Monkees albums charted simultaneously. Soon the group had one of the biggest tours of the year. The one setback to this incredible turn of events was that now that the reunion tour looked set to run indefinitely, Nesmith could no longer participate.

Few could fault Nesmith, who was now consumed with running his Pacific Arts home-video production company, producing the major motion pictures *Square*

Dance and *Tape Heads*, and managing the multimillion-dollar estate of his late mother, Bette Nesmith (the inventor of Liquid Paper). Proving his good faith toward the reunion, Nesmith did eventually join Tork, Dolenz, and Jones for an MTV Christmas video, as well as encore performances of "Listen To The Band" and "Pleasant Valley Sunday" at Los Angeles' Greek Theater on September 7, 1986.

Micky, Davy, and Peter's reunion of 1986 spilled into 1987 with another tour and an all-new album called *Pool It!* The first single from it was the catchy "Heart And Soul," a song discovered by British producer Roger Bechirian. A first-class music video was produced to accompany the single, yet mysteriously it would never appear on MTV. After several months of frustration it was discovered that The Monkees, unbeknownst to their manager or record label, had been blacklisted by the station executives after a misunderstanding over a guest appearance. Even after restricted documents reflecting the video's unquestionable popularity with MTV's audience were made public via industry trade papers, the network still refused to grant airtime. Two tours followed *Pool It!*, but each drew lower attendance figures than the previous one. No longer able to get the kind of quality bookings they formerly enjoyed, Dolenz, Jones, and Tork let The Monkees' legacy rest, roadwise, for seven years.

With time to recover and reflect, the individual Monkees approached their 30th anniversary in 1996 with varying degrees of expectation. An incredible peak to an already extraordinary career had been reached in 1986, and it was believed that 1996 could be even bigger, if strategically planned. To facilitate a close working relationship within the group, *Monkees* veteran Ward Sylvester was appointed to man age all four band members. Aside from the obligatory tour, it was hoped that the group would once again collaborate in the studio.

Slowly and secretively, Michael, Micky, and Peter began hashing out tunes at a rehearsal room in Hollywood, soon to be joined by Davy. In no time they were back together recording with far-reaching plans to perform and produce a new album. It would not be easy. Group meetings were a constant necessity, and although the record was fully funded by Rhino Records, the band demanded that there be no outside interference until it was complete. The result was *Justus*, a highly ambitious offering.

Photo: Jay Silverman

The following year all four band members toured England, sat for interviews for the first-ever Monkees documentary, and produced and starred in a reprise of their TV show for the ABC network, which became the group's first prime-time special in 27 years. The Monkees toured that summer, but Nesmith elected not to join them.

It seems that The Monkees will continue to tour from time to time, and, on occasion, participate in worthwhile projects, while Rhino will continue to seek out more of the group's missing tapes and produce new releases of the highest quality, such as *The Headquarters Sessions*.

Despite all the personal and personnel shake-ups The Monkees have experienced through the years, the bond that the bandmates forged remains eternal. "The four of us had such a good thing going," says a wistful Jones. "We all had egos, but we had one thing in mind at the end of the day—that we all ended up together, bowing at the same time."

These notes in part previously appeared in *The Monkees' Anthology* (Rhino).

Song Stories From
The Guys Who Sang 'Em

and
The Guys Who Wrote 'Em

1. (THEME FROM) THE MONKEES

Disc 1
1966

Boyce & Hart's "(Theme From) The Monkees" is a remarkable composition in that it encapsulates the essence of The Monkees and their show before there was such a thing. Nonetheless, the song reportedly embarrassed the group members, who thought it sounded like "Hey, hey we're The Beatles." Moreover, the lyric "Come and watch us sing and play" would take on new meaning when the group was refused permission to be involved instrumentally in their own recording sessions. Consequently, the song has never been performed in concert, the group opting instead for a prerecorded tape as their intro. Unbeknownst to the band, it was not really The Beatles who inspired the song, but rather the purveyors of the Tottenham Sound.

Bobby Hart (songwriter): "*The Monkees'* theme was influenced by a Dave Clark Five song called 'Catch Us If You Can.' They had that finger-snapping thing. Tommy and I lived on the same street at that time, and we wrote that walking down to the park on Cahuenga Boulevard by Barham. It's really a walking beat, and we decided that would be great to write to."

Photo courtesy of Andrew Sandoval Collection

2. I WANNA BE FREE (Fast Version)

This up-tempo folk-rock version of "I Wanna Be Free" was featured in the pilot episode of *The Monkees* television series. However, this take did not originally appear on an album and was exclusive to the show's soundtrack until 1990, when it was released on the rarities collection *Missing Links Volume Two*. It is one of Bobby Hart's favorite Monkees compositions.

Bobby Hart: "That's one of the few songs in my whole career, certainly with Boyce, that we wrote just because we felt like writing one night. Usually we were writing for pro

jects all the time. This was one evening when Tommy and I were sharing a house in the Hollywood Hills, and he just said, 'I have this idea—do you feel like writing something?' There was a line that was inspired by a Roger Miller song—a ballad about suicide, basically. It may have had the words 'I wanna be free' in it. We just started with the title, and it kind of flowed out. He sang me, 'I wanna be free . . .' and I went on into, 'like the bluebirds flying by me.' We had the whole thing wrapped up in less than an hour. It was one of those few times we did it for the fun of it."[1]

3. LET'S DANCE ON

Written specifically for the pilot episode's dance sequence, "Let's Dance On" is a Monkees party number that owes a debt to such songs as "Twist And Shout" and "La Bamba." A raw Boyce & Hart production, with a great and gritty garage-band Vox organ solo from Bobby, this recording is also notable for the complete lack of bass guitar.

Bobby Hart: "We probably should have spent more time on that."

Historical note: Another version of "Let's Dance On" was recorded a month earlier, on June 10, 1966, by producer Snuff Garrett. However, the tracks were scrapped when

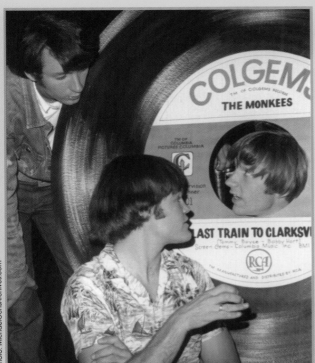

Photo: MichaelOchsArchives.com

Garrett clashed with The Monkees over who should sing the song's lead vocal.

4. LAST TRAIN TO CLARKSVILLE

Inspired by the fade-out of The Beatles' "Paperback Writer," "Last Train To Clarksville" was The Monkees' first single, released on August 16, 1966. Predating the television series' debut by almost a month, this record was the world's introduction to Mike, Micky, Davy, and Peter. Surprisingly, "Clarksville" was written only a few weeks beforehand as album filler.

Bobby Hart: "I had it in the back of my mind, and then we were coming down to the end of producing the first album. We needed another song or two. I guess an album had to have 12 songs in those days. We didn't know that there were going to be two Nesmith songs on the album, so we were trying to come up with 12 on our own. I said I had this idea, and Tommy and I got together and did it really quickly."

ASK FOR "THE MONKEES" LP ALBUM

The song is also notable for its underlying theme of going off to war.

Bobby Hart: "That was inherent in the thing. We couldn't be too direct with The Monkees; we couldn't really make a protest song out of it. We kind of snuck it in subtly. We didn't know at that time that there is an air force base near the town of Clarksville, Tennessee. We were just looking for a name that sounded good. There's a little town in northern Arizona I used to go through in the summers on the way to Oak Creek Canyon called Clarksdale. We were throwing out some names, and then when we got to Clarksdale we stopped there for a minute and thought *That sounded pretty good.* We thought Clarksville would maybe be even a little better. I did a demo of it sometime in the '70s that included a recitation about the war. We also cut a follow-up to 'Last Train To Clarksville' with a girl named Linda Ball. It was a slight variation of the lyric: 'He's on the last train to Clarksville.'"

5. TAKE A GIANT STEP

Gerry Goffin & Carole King's "Take A Giant Step" was one of Don Kirshner's selections for The Monkees. It was first issued in August '66 as the flip side to "Last Train To Clarksville" and was later included on the band's first album.

Bobby Hart: "Once the show was sold, that's when Donnie got involved. Tommy and I had been working for about a year or more doing the demos for the pilot and getting it all together. Then all of a sudden everybody was serious, and Donnie was on the next plane with a stack of demos under his arm. He felt strongly about certain ones. We were told to do 'Take A Giant Step,' 'I'll Be True To You,' and 'Saturday's Child.' We basically got his permission to do the other songs that we had written. Nesmith was off in another studio doing his stuff and putting pressure on (Kirshner) to be represented. Not to downplay Donnie's part in the whole thing. He had real specific ideas of what he wanted in the album—not so much the sound of the records. He had all these formulas. He was

Tommy Boyce & Bobby Hart

Jerry Goffin, Carole King & Neil Sedaka

always making lists and notes narrowing down the reasons why this should go in and this should go out—that kind of stuff. He was good at that."

Historical note: "Take A Giant Step" was another song originally attempted by producer Snuff Garrett. According to Garrett, his production was to have featured Davy on lead vocals. When Boyce & Hart replaced Garrett a producers, they recut the song with Micky singing lead.

The Monkees with Don Kirshner

6. ALL THE KING'S HORSES

Michael Nesmith's "All The King's Horses" hails from his first Monkees recording session as a producer. Although the song was used in two episodes of the television show, it never originally saw release on a record. The track was later exhumed fo

Missing Links, Volume Two, which features other rarities from the television show sound track.

Michael Nesmith: "That was part of an original rock trio that I was in called Mike, Joh

& Bill. 'All The King's Horses' was just one of the songs that I was writing for that trio."

Historical note: Nesmith formed Mike, John & Bill shortly after he moved to Los Angeles in 1964. The group consisted of Nesmith as guitarist and vocalist, bassist John London (who became Nesmith's stand-in on the series), and drummer Bill Sleeper. The trio issued one fantastic single on Frankie Laine's Omnibus label ("How Can You Kiss Me?" c/w "Just A Little Love") in 1964, but, sadly, fell apart when Bill Sleeper was drafted.

7. SATURDAY'S CHILD

Another Kirshner selection (perhaps prompted by West Coast Screen Gems head Lester Sill), "Saturday's Child" was written by David Gates. Gates began writing songs in the late '50s, and by the time of "Saturday's Child" he had racked up an impressive array of credits, including work with Chuck Berry, Elvis Presley, and Bobby Darin. Gates later went on to form the group Bread.

David Gates (songwriter): "I had known Davy Jones and produced a session with him before The Monkees—a really nice guy. I also knew Michael Nesmith before the group—also a really good guy and a very talented musician. I was a staff writer at Screen Gems when The Monkees were being formed. 'Saturday's Child' had been under consideration for their first single, but they put out 'Last Train To Clarksville' instead."

Historical note: Around the same time that The Monkees cut "Saturday's Child," Herman's Hermits recorded a similar version of the song for their *There's A Kind Of Hush All Over The World* album. Micky Most, the producer of Herman's Hermits, had actually turned down the opportunity to produce The Monkees around the same time as this session. It is possible that "Saturday's Child" was one of the perspective songs he had been asked to cut for The Monkees project. Most also recorded Boyce & Hart's "If You're Thinkin' What I'm Thinkin'" during that period, leading to further speculation about whether these tracks may have been originally intended for The Monkees.

8. PAPA GENE'S BLUES

"Papa Gene's Blues" is a Michael Nesmith song that dates back to his days as Michael Blessing—an acoustic guitar-strumming and harmonica-blowing folkie, à la Bob Dylan.

Michael Nesmith: "A 'Different Drum' period song, far pre-Monkees. I brought that into The Monkees' environment. The *Gene* should be spelled *Jean.* It refers to a girl that went to school with whose name was Jean."

Historical note: Recorded under the working title "Brand X," this song is notable for the inclusion of Peter Tork on acoustic guitar—the first Monkee to appear instrumentally on a "Monkees" recording. Ironically, even Nesmith did not play on his own early tracks, as he was consumed with his role as producer on these sessions.

9. I WANNA BE FREE (Album Version)

Recorded the same day as the "fast" version, this ballad take of "I Wanna Be Free" was included on The Monkees' self-titled debut album, released in October 1966. The Boyce & Hart song, which became a trademark for Davy Jones, features a lovely, albeit uncredited, string arrangement by Don McGinnis.

Bobby Hart: "He was in the office every day, and we were encouraged to try him by Lester Sill. He turned out to be great with whatever we asked him to do. He did nice, nice work. We told him we wanted a 'Yesterday'-type string-quartet arrangement, and he came right in with it."

Micky Dolenz: "I remember wanting to sing 'I Wanna Be Free.' I really loved it, but I had too many songs on the album. Davy became the balladeer."

10. SWEET YOUNG THING

Michael Nesmith's second cut on The Monkees' first album emanated from a one-off collaboration with master songsmiths Goffin & King. This teaming was suggested by Kirshner, who had hoped it would produce a more commercial sound from Nesmith

Michael Nesmith: "I think 'Sweet Young Thing' was a good song. I liked Gerry and Carole quite a bit. It was not the sort of songwriting alliance that I would continue to any great effect. You know, I'm just not a big fan of their songs. Well, that's not true. I am sort of a fan of their songs. I was not a fan of the writing environment. I didn't like being cast in with some other folks and being told, 'Write with them.' Gerry and Carole had very strong songwriting styles. I really enjoyed working with them; it was just the circumstances that were tough."

Historical note: Like Micky Most and Snuff Garrett, Goffin & King had originally been offered a shot at producing The Monkees. However, after writing "Sweet Young Thing" with Nesmith, the duo clashed in the studio with Michael. They returned to New York without completing any recordings for the first album.

11. GONNA BUY ME A DOG

Recorded toward the end of the first album sessions, Boyce & Hart's "Gonna Buy Me A Dog" had already been attempted at an earlier Nesmith session but was left incomplete. Similarly, Boyce & Hart's production could barely be perceived as a finished one. Nevertheless, the freewheeling spirit of Micky and Davy's loose performance made the song a group favorite, managing to capture the irreverence of their TV show on record.

Micky Dolenz: "Originally that was supposed to be done straight. Davy and I just started goofing on it, and they ended up using the goof rather than the straight version. That happened an awful lot in the television show. They would use the outtakes."

Bobby Hart: "We were trying to follow the whole Beatles formula all the way. What Bob and Bert had told us in our first meeting with them was, 'We're going to do an American Beatles for television.' So that's basically the way we looked at The Monkees project. We tailored the whole album that way. 'I Wanna Be Free' was our 'Yesterday' with a string quartet. (With 'Gonna Buy Me A Dog') we felt like we needed a novelty cut, à la the Ringo Starr cuts on The Beatles' albums. They didn't understand the song; they thought it was real stupid. They were just basically making fun of it. That's what usually happened when there were at least two of them in the same room. They would try and outdo each other with cutting up. We thought it was great and kept the jokes in."

12. I DON'T THINK YOU KNOW ME (First Recorded Version)

Although his collaboration with Goffin & King quickly turned sour, Nesmith managed to squeeze more than just "Sweet Young Thing" out of the short-lived union. In particular, "I Don't Think You Know Me" was a song that Goffin & King were eager to cut with The Monkees, and that is most likely the reason why Nesmith produced his own recording of the tune in June 1966. Not only was it an excellent vehicle for his vocal and production style, but the song also served as a blueprint for the arrangement of his classic "You Just May Be The One." The similarity of the songs was not apparent at the time, because no Monkees version of "I Don't Think You Know Me" was heard until 1987's *Missing Links* compilation.

Historical note: Later in 1966 Goffin & King got another chance to produce The Monkees with the tracks to be cut in New York without the group's involvement. "I Don't Think You Know Me" was rerecorded with lead vocals by Peter and a version with both Davy and Peter singing. Neither was deemed fit for consumption at the time, and the Peter-sung version was later included as a bonus track on the reissue of *More Of The Monkees*.

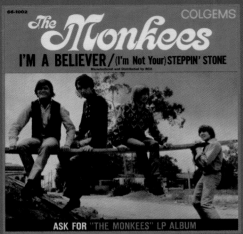

13. I'M A BELIEVER

Neil Diamond's "I'm A Believer" is The Monkees' most popular song of all time. As a single it was one of the most eagerly anticipated releases of the 1960s. Astonishingly, more than a million copies of the 45 were sold in advance without buyers ever hearing a note. "I'm A Believer" was also the first Monkees release to be cut on the East Coast by producer Jeff Barry.

Neil Diamond (songwriter): "'Cherry Cherry' was my second chart record, and that caught Don Kirshner's ear. Don Kirshner liked the song very much and asked if I had something The Monkees could do. So I sent them over my version of 'I'm A Believer.' It was originally a song that I wrote for my second album. It was a simple self-expression, happy kind of thing. I didn't think too much of it. I just liked the title—that's how the song came. I was involved a little bit in the mixing of it, which Jeff Barry did with Don Kirshner. I remember we did it late at night and had it finished by deadline. It was very exciting because we knew 'I'm A Believer' was gonna go all the way. For me it was particularly exciting because I was in a recording room with Don Kirshner, who two years before I couldn't get an appointment with. Now I'm sharing what will be the biggest hit of the year with him and Jeff Barry, who was one of my idols. As a songwriter I was very pleased about having them do it. Of course, when I reported back to Bert Berns, who was head of (my label) Bang Records, that I had allowed The Monkees to try the song out, he went ballistic. He felt it would have been a giant hit for me. But I think they did a great job with it, and I have no regrets at all."

14. (I'M NOT YOUR) STEPPIN' STONE

Boyce & Hart were slowly getting edged out of their production role by Don Kirshner

Neil Diamond

and show creator Bert Schneider. It was Schneider's assertion that Boyce & Hart were cutting too much material of questionable commerciality. Meanwhile, Don Kirshner enjoyed making records closer to home in New York City, and therefore he preferred to work with East Coast producers such as Jeff Barry. In spite of that, it was hard to question Boyce & Hart's songwriting prowess and commercial instincts on "(I'm Not Your) Steppin' Stone." As a high-charting flip side of "I'm A Believer," the tune gained considerable exposure and became one of The Monkees' trademark songs. It is also one of Boyce & Hart's most covered compositions, with recordings ranging from The Sex Pistols to Paul Revere & The Raiders.

Bobby Hart: "'Steppin' Stone' was written ahead of time. We were thinking of Paul Revere & The Raiders when we wrote it. It was the biggest garage band song we ever wrote. It seems like a lot of kids cut their teeth on that. It was easy changes. I don't know what else. Maybe that was the biggest reason: the changes were easy."

15. SHE

Another unquestionably classic Boyce & Hart track, "She" is one of only two songs that Kirshner selected from the duo for inclusion on the group's second album, *More Of The Monkees*. This was unfortunate because Boyce & Hart had almost an entire album's worth of solid material already in the can. Prolificity aside, in interviews Tommy and Bobby would often boast of their ability to come up with songs in the most unlikely places. Case in point: "She" was supposedly written in a library. Bobby Hart later said that these claims were not entirely true.

Bobby Hart: "It wasn't actually in a library. . . . We often went to the park on nice days to write outside. We'd sit on the grass with Tommy's guitar and a pad and pencil. This was another song that we had written before The Monkees project. It was during the period when some of the groups playing on the Strip in L.A. were like The Leaves. Several local groups were experimenting with a kind of psychedelic rock. It never really made it nationally. The Doors were the ones that did. We were hanging out on the Strip a lot in those days and were inspired by these psychedelic trends that were happening."

16. MARY, MARY

In a bid to appease his increasing demand for musical autonomy, Michael Nesmith was allotted his standard two cuts on *More Of The Monkees.* In particular, "Mary, Mary" was used as an example of the group's musical role in their records when a reporter from *Look* magazine was invited to watch Michael produce Micky, Davy, and Peter overdubbing backing vocals onto the song. The outcome was predictably chaotic: Mike and Peter argued, while Micky and Davy spent most of the evening clowning around, singing things like "'Mary, Mary' written by Mike Nesmith, copyright 1966 by Screen Gems." Meanwhile, Don Kirshner and Lester Sill, who were seated on either side of Mike at the controls, kept a watchful eye on the proceedings. The caption for the photo included in *Look* contains the classic Nesmith quote: "These guys from New York, they bug me." Although the results of the night's recording were deemed unusable, Lester Sill told *Look*: "It'll be okay. If you gotta girl's name, you got a lot goin' for you. Think of how many Marys there are."

Michael Nesmith: "The Monkees' version was one of the early studio bands coming together. Glen Campbell played the guitar part. That was really a blues lick that I had wanted to incorporate in a very straight-ahead blues type of song. He just had the dickens of a time gettin' it because he was a country player, not a blues player. So i ended up with The Monkees' version flavoring the thing off into the country vein. In addition, the L.A. session players were off into the country vein as well. At the end o the day the version that I like of it best is Paul Butterfield's."

17. YOUR AUNTIE GRIZELDA

After sitting on the sidelines for most of the group's early sessions, Peter Tork wa finally given a lead vocal role on Jack Keller and Diane Hilderbrand's "Your Auntie Grizelda." Originally offered to Tork by Screen Gems' Lester Sill as a protest number to suit his folk background, "Grizelda" was in reality the silliest "19th Nervous Breakdown sound-alike ever! Predictably, Tork did not appreciate the song's novelty flavor, thoug he would later establish a creative link with Hilderbrand.

Jack Keller (songwriter): "That was the first song that Diane and I wrote together. We were introduced by Lester Sill in 1966, and we were kind of surprised it ended up bein done the way it was. I thought The Monks would cut it like '19th Nervous Breakdown with Micky singing lead, or Micky and Davy. It turned out to be a total surprise to me when it came to the session, and Jeff Barry said, 'Peter's going to sing it.' It was a total comedy thing. He did that all in one take—no second take, that was it. He made up the whole thing. I was in a total state of shock when I heard it."

Peter Tork: "Lester came to me and said, 'We've got a kind of a protest song for you.' It certainly isn't what you call a protest song. That was what they thought a protest song should be for The Monkees. I believe it was Jeff Barry (who) got me to do that. He had me doin' those funny vocal things in the middle there. I tried it, and it worked out—*kind of.*"

Jack Keller

Jack Keller: "The tracks were recorded at American Studios, where Three Dog Night used to record with Richie Podolor, who was the engineer. At that time The Monkees were only dealing with Jeff Barry. So Donnie said, 'Hey, do you mind if you split the production with Jeff? Because he can get Davy to come in and sing.' I didn't know that he was going to use Peter on 'Your Auntie Grizelda.' '19th Nervous Breakdown' went right out the door, but I got used to it. Over the years it became a #1 on *Dr. Demento*, and so I thought, 'Well, this is pretty cool.' Now my kids like it. To this day it's one of the good ones."

18. OF YOU (Previously Unissued Mix)

"Of You" was written by brothers Bill and John Chadwick and originally copyrighted on October 28, 1965. Bill Chadwick was a bandmate of Michael Nesmith's in 1965 and had actually auditioned for a part in *The Monkees* alongside Michael. When Chadwick missed out on a role, he remained close to the project, writing songs,

Bill Chadwick in The Elementary School Band
L to R: **Fred Olsen, Mick Tani, Bill Chadwick, James Hendrix & Jim Voit**

playing on sessions, and traveling with The Monkees. Nesmith actually recorded "Of You" the very same hour that Boyce & Hart were cutting "Last Train To Clarksville" at another studio a few blocks away. Although the song was not released at the time, Nesmith did return to the track in 1969 to replace his old lead vocal. "Of You" first appeared on *Missing Links*, but this box set marks the first release of the song's original 1966 mix.

Davy Jones: "Mike Nesmith had a problem for the first year and a half. He was singing like it was coming out of his nose. During the course of *The Monkees'* first year he had his tonsils out. If you listen to it, it's very nasal, very throaty. It all sounded as if he had a cushion in his throat. That was why he had a different quality when he went on to do his later stuff. He had 'em out, (and) his vocal presentation changed."

Michael Nesmith: "My tonsils were so big that if you listen to the first episodes it all sounds like that."

19. LOOK OUT (HERE COMES TOMORROW)
(Previously Unissued Extended Version)
Neil Diamond's "Look Out (Here Comes Tomorrow)," included on *More Of The Monkees*, was frequently featured on the group's television series. One particular episode, "The Monkees In Manhattan," features a longer mix of the song, and it is now included on this box set.

Neil Diamond: "That was just one of the two or three things of mine that they recorded. All of my songs then were basically built around four or five chords. That's just my style of writing. I hoped it would become a hit, but it ended up on an album I don't think it was ever released as a single."

20. THE KIND OF GIRL I COULD LOVE
"The Kind Of Girl I Could Love" was another attempt by Screen Gems to steer Michael Nesmith's talents down a more commercial avenue by teaming him with another more pop-oriented writer. The song was actually cut during the first album sessions and was cowritten with Roger Atkins. As it turned out, Atkins (best known for composing such hits as The Animals' "It's My Life" and The 5th Dimension's "Workin' On A Groovy Thing") yielded an intriguing, yet decidedly uncommercial Latin-country blend from Nesmith.

21. SOMETIME IN THE MORNING
Although Goffin & King penned at least two submissions for *More Of The Monkees*, the one that made it onto the record was the sublime "Sometime In The Morning." Like many of the second album's cuts, the backing track for "Sometime In The Morning" was recorded in New York—without The Monkees' involvement—and lat-

shipped out to Los Angeles for completion. On this particular track, Carole King sent a separate multitrack tape with her performing the three-part vocal arrangement for The Monkees to replicate for the final master. While the group was always grateful for King's excellent material, mimicking another artist's performance left little room for input from them as performers.

Hank Cicalo (engineer): "In those days, you used to get a demo, and when Carole and Gerry sent us one it would have everything built into it. A hell of a performance, some great hook—something that made it really great. Inevitably, anyone who ever did a Carole King demo would duplicate it. You had to, because that was what made that demo great. Sometimes you'd get into situations where you're trying to do something that's not really you. But that's what Screen Gems would want them to do: 'Gee, sing it just like Gerry sang that verse.' I found at times they were forced into things that were difficult to deal with."

22. WHEN LOVE COMES KNOCKIN' (AT YOUR DOOR)

This song sprang from a collaboration between Carole Bayer and Neil Sedaka. Another track with New York origins, it was one of the final recordings completed for *More Of The Monkees*. The song's last verse features a hook borrowed from another Sedaka hit, "Breaking Up Is Hard To Do," in which a second voice sings a counter melody to the lead.

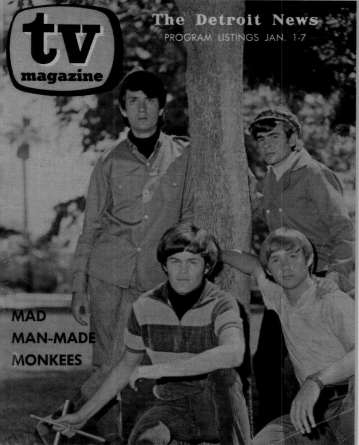

Neil Sedaka (songwriter): "I love to sing with myself, and I loved having the two melodies going at once. I thought that was innovative at the time for a pop song. I thought that Davy Jones was very professional and very charming. Carol was delightful to work with, a gorgeous girl. As a matter of fact, Davy Jones had quite a crush on her."

23. DO NOT ASK FOR LOVE (First Recorded Version)

Michael Murphey, a friend of Michael Nesmith's from Dallas, wrote the beautiful "D[o] Not Ask For Love." It had originally been composed for a group called The Ne[w] Society, who recorded it on an album for RCA Records. Interestingly, The New Societ[y] actually evolved out of another group known as The Survivors, a large folk ensembl[e] featuring Nesmith with Murphey, Bill Chadwick, Owen Castleman, and John Londo[n] among other notables. Unfortunately, The Monkees' version languished in the can un[til] *Missing Links, Volume Two.* Murphey, Castleman, and London later teamed up as Th[e] Monkees' Colgems labelmates The Lewis & Clarke Expedition.

Historical note: In late 1968 a second Monkees version of this song (under the tit[le] "Prithee") was cut by Peter Tork and producer Bones Howe for The Monkees televisio[n] special *33 1/3 Revolutions Per Monkee.*

24. VALLERI (First Recorded Version)

The original version of "Valleri" was perhaps Boyce & Hart's finest hour with Th[e] Monkees. The song was a surefire hit with a great guitar solo from Louie Shelton. [It] was recorded in August 1966, in time to be a part of the *More Of The Monkees* albu[m,] but possibly held back by Kirshner as a potential single. Nevertheless, after th[e] song received a couple of airings on the television show, it remained in the ca[n,] apparently the victim of the brewing struggle between Kirshner and The Monkees.

Davy Jones & Jeff Barry

Photo courtesy of Andrew Sandoval

Bobby Hart: "'Valleri' was specifical[ly] written for them. We actually wrote [it] in the car going up Mulholland fro[m] Woodrow Wilson and Laurel Canyo[n] over to the house that (Kirshner) w[as] renting in the suburbs. We cut th[e] song just prior to the point where w[e] were dismissed as producers. Th[e] first was a better version."

25. I'LL BE BACK UPON M[Y] FEET (First Recorded Version)

Another incredible track that f[ell] afoul of the Kirshner/Monkees fe[ud] is "I'll Be Back Upon My Fee[t." This *More Of The Monkees*-e[ra] recording was featured a few tim[es] on the show before being shelve[d.] Although the group seemed to li[ke] it, going so far as to attempt a ne[w] version during sessions for *Pisces, Aquarius, Capricorn & Jones Ltd.* (with Michael Nesmith on guitar), no finished takes were completed. Ironically, by the time the group got around to recording a releasable take, they had returned to using session men for musical backing, which was the whole reason why this original version had gone unused.

Disc 2 1967 1. A LITTLE BIT ME, A LITTLE BIT YOU

The final straw in The Monkees' musical showdown with Kirshner, "A Little Bit Me, A Little Bit You" was the single that broke the camel's back. By issuing this record without the band and Raybert Productions' permission, Kirshner found himself ousted from The Monkees project. Kirshner immediately sued Columbia Pictures for $35.5 million dollars, and the single was recalled. It would be reissued weeks later with a different flip side.

Neil Diamond: "It sounds more like a Neil Diamond kind of song. I would guess that it was something that I had started and thought that they might be able to do or like. I was not involved in the session at all; as a matter of fact, I've never met The Monkees. I've always been very thankful to them because they helped pay for my kid's braces! I have a wing of my house dedicated to them."

2. SHE HANGS OUT (Single Version)

At the heart of Kirshner's dismissal was his refusal to include a Monkees-performed recording on one side of the band's third single. Unfortunately, Kirshner felt obligated to give Neil Diamond the A-side of the record after the success of "I'm A Believer." Moreover, producer Jeff Barry probably wanted another slice of the pie. "She Hangs Out" was originally slated as the flip side to "A Little Bit Me, A Little Bit You." It is possible that the song was first circulated on a custom-pressed promotional single manufactured by Don Kirshner at the beginning of February 1967. This single's label read: "MY FAVORITE MONKEE" DAVY JONES SINGS. This was not only an overt reference to Jones' apparent loyalty to the Svengali, but a testament to Kirshner's assertion that he could "do it without them." The "them" being Mike, Peter, and Micky, and the "do it" meaning record and release Monkees records regardless of whom they featured. In Canada this single somehow managed to make it to the stores as a standard release (without the "FAVORITE MONKEE" business on the label). But the rest of the world wouldn't hear the song until the group's rerecording was released on November 1967's *Pisces, Aquarius, Capricorn & Jones Ltd.*

3. THE GIRL I KNEW SOMEWHERE

"The Girl I Knew Somewhere" wound up as the flip side of commercially released copies of "A Little Bit Me, A Little Bit You." It hails from the second-ever recording session to feature The Monkees singing and playing as a group. At their first group session a month earlier, The Monkees had tried the song with Michael on lead vocals, but the results were turned down for release. The purpose of the second version, included here, was to record a new take with Micky singing lead, ensuring the song's chance for single release.

Chip Douglas (producer): "It was Lester Sill's feeling that Micky should sing it. Probably Bert and Bob's too. It never occurred to me because it was Mike's song. Lester must have suggested, 'Well, get Micky to sing it, and we'll put it out as a single.'"

"The Girl I Knew Somewhere" was one of Michael Nesmith's breeziest pieces and worked especially well in the group dynamic.

Michael Nesmith: "That was out of the 'You Just May Be The One' mold. An attempt to write pop songs that might be playable by the group as a band."

Peter Tork: "It's one of Mike's better ones of the era. I remember the harpsichord solo. I had the general idea for a while, and then Mike was in my dressing room, and I played him what I had for it. I was noodling around with it. Then we hit that discord at the downbeat at the end of the solo, and I hadn't meant to do that. I said, 'What was that?' Mike said, 'I heard it, I heard it.' I tried it again—it just seemed to be locked into my hands. We were tickled to death to have this funny note. It disappeared in the record. You know the harpsichord did not work too terribly well in pop music. It was just something that I wanted to do because I am partly a classicist. I believe in the old stuff. Bach was already by that time my favorite composer, so harpsichords were *the thing*. I had one on the TV show episode with Julie Newmar; they mounted on a bicycle."

4. ALL OF YOUR TOYS

Bill Martin's "All Of Your Toys" was cut in January 1967 at the first group recording session, and it was hoped that it too would become a single release. However,

Jim Dickson and Eddie Tickner (managers of The Byrds among other artists) owned the song's publishing rights, and the two refused to sell the song outright to Screen Gems. Screen Gems in turn refused to release anything they could not wholly own.

Chip Douglas: "We thought that was going to be a great single. I got real excited when Bill Martin showed it to me. I said, 'Hey, this would be great.' I

Chip Douglas & Bill Martin

Photo: Henry Diltz

didn't realize at the time that it didn't have a chorus. I probably would have written one had I had the chance to do it today. It was the kind of song that didn't quite finish off right; it kind of goes into this rip-off of the 'Paperback Writer' build-up thing in the middle, with the ascending 'ahs.'"

5. LOVE TO LOVE

Neil Diamond's "Love To Love" was taped at the New York sessions for "A Little Bit Me, A Little Bit You" and was ultimately shelved when Kirshner was fired. In August 1969 the backing track was dusted off by music coordinator Brendan Cahill, who supervised Davy Jones' double-tracking of a new lead vocal onto the two-year-old recording. Work never progressed beyond this point, and "Love To Love" was not originally issued. In the early '70s a rough mix of the song escaped the vault, eventually turning up on the 1979 Australian-only compilation *Monkeemania*.

Neil Diamond: "I never heard them do it. You know honestly, I don't ever remember sending it to The Monkees or The Monkees ever recording it. It may have been one of the songs I was writing for one of my albums that Jeff tried with them."

6. YOU TOLD ME

Michael Nesmith's "You Told Me" kicked off The Monkees' first "group-only" album, *Headquarters*. The song's bass line and mock frantic count-off were inspired by The Beatles' *Revolver* album opener, "Taxman."

Peter Tork: "The opening is satirical of 'Taxman.' That's the one with the banjo. Very interesting use of banjo on that cut—thought it really kicked it. I suppose anybody listening to it would sort of automatically throw that into a country bag in their mind but I always thought that that was just a pretty 'rock-y' use of the banjo. My friends a said, 'That's your ax, buddy.' I think that it just really kills when the banjo comes in righ in the middle of that, and the band hits with that nice bass drop. I think in some way that one moment whips the other to albums to hell. Tommy and Bobby were reall experts at doing what they did, and Donnie was an expert at doing what he did, bu none of those guys were really interested in how music is just exciting in and of itself

7. I'LL SPEND MY LIFE WITH YOU

Boyce & Hart's "I'll Spend My Life With You," a Kirshner reject from the *More Of Th Monkees* sessions, was rerecorded for *Headquarters*. With a great production cou tesy of Chip Douglas, the band's agile performance makes this second versio clearly superior.

Tommy Boyce (songwriter): "We wrote that in the office. In those days I was a b confused about women in general. This particular girl—she left me for a gangste actually, a New York gangster. Bobby helped me finish it, and I played it for her thin ing it would maybe get her to stay with me. Of course she left."

Peter Tork: "I liked 'Spend My Life With You.' I managed to talk to Tommy about that. was one of the few real songs he wrote, because there really was somebody. You ca tell, you know, that the song is real heartfelt. Something about it is not jacked-up an forced. Did you notice, incidentally, there were no traps on that song—there's not drum kit on it. The rhythm section is Micky playing backbeats on the guitar and Dav on the tambourine. Michael was taking a few pedal steel lessons. I would not like have seen us be a country music band, but I love the idea of Michael playing ped steel. He's a very powerful guy in a lot of ways."

8. FORGET THAT GIRL

Prior to his production debut on *Headquarters*, Chip Douglas had played bass with such groups as The Turtles, Modern Folk Quintet, and The Gene Clark Group. He contributed his song "Forget That Girl" to the *Headquarters* project, a selection that did not originally meet with Kirshner's approval.

Chip Douglas: "I'd showed it to Kirshner, and his comment was, 'It kind of has a negative message, don't you think?' I was really taken aback. I'd never thought about it that way. It was kind of advice to myself. I was crazy about

a girl who had this other guy that she was crazy about. I knew it was never going to work out. I had real mixed feelings when we did that because no one could pick up on the original riff that I had worked out for it. I had gone with (The Turtles') Mark Volman into Harmony Recorders, and we made this little demo of it. It was more like 'Rescue Me' from Fontella Bass. I was hoping it would sound Motown. Nobody could get the hang of that riff because of the way it started. It didn't start on the downbeat; t was a couple of beats before the downbeat. It turned out a lot more bubblegum han I had hoped."

Peter Tork: "I thought that was a pretty good song, actually. He's a pretty sophisticated musician, but I've heard places where his sophistication just totally ran away with him. This was not a case where that happened. I was pleasantly surprised. I like the changes, and I like the lyric too. It was fun to do."

9. YOU JUST MAY BE THE ONE

Michael Nesmith's "You Just May Be The One" proved to be the group highlight of *Headquarters*. Captured in just two takes, the results are pop perfection. The song dates back to Nesmith's days as a folk artist performing at the Troubadour club in West Hollywood.

Chip Douglas: "That's when I first got to know him; he knew me more than I knew him. I saw him with Bill Chadwick doing 'You Just May Be The One.' That is the one song that I remember I was real impressed with. I remember those harmonies—Bill Chadwick hitting that high A note (on the bridge). I thought, *Wow, that sounds neat*. So when the song came up for suggestion to put on the album, I said, 'Yeah, that's great! Can we do that same harmony like you guys used to do it?' He said, 'Sure, Micky will do it.'"

Peter Tork: "It has two bars of five in the middle of it, which Mike didn't know he'd written. I mean, I told him that, and he just didn't take it in because he never listened to me. Somebody else told him, and he came at me yelling, 'Look what I did!' It was a good Mike song."

Historical note: Michael Nesmith produced an earlier version of "You Just May Be The One" during sessions for the first Monkees album. Like many other tracks from this period, this first version appeared on the television soundtrack only and was unissued until the release of *Missing Links, Volume Two* in 1990.

10. SHADES OF GRAY

Another *Headquarters* highlight is Barry Mann & Cynthia Weil's "Shades Of Gray." Vocally, the song features a graceful blend of Davy, Peter, and Micky's voices. Musically, it boasts a baroque string and horn arrangement courtesy of Mike and Peter.

Chip Douglas: "I guess the vocal arrangement was pretty much my idea. There wo some collaboration that went on. I'm sure we tossed it around, but I generally alwa tried to get them to sing together. Put harmony parts onto each other. We just starte somewhere with Davy and continued and added more parts as we went along."

Peter Tork: "Great song. We were just thrilled to death with that. We created th arrangement ourselves from scratch. I don't remember what kind of a demo the gave us. Mike wrote the horn and cello parts, and I notated them. Mike basical wrote the counterpoint stuff in his head. It was great to have him do that and to kn how to tell a French horn player what to do. I created that piano intro. I thought, k the time I got it done, *This is one of my favorite things I've ever done.*"

Photo: MichaelOchsArchives.com

Barry Mann & Cynthia We

Historical note: The August 12 issue of *Billboard* reported that "Shades Of Gray" was be released as a single after strong airplay in regional markets such as Milwauke However, no single was ever released from *Headquarters* in the United States.

Peter Tork: "My only regret is that we couldn't generate a bona fide single off of th album in this country. 'Shades Of Gray,' I guess, has been deemed to be the hit fro that, sort of an album hit."

Chip Douglas: "Micky's song was maybe going to be the single. There was some to about it, but I guess it just wound up having no single. They thought, 'Well, we'll just s the album, we don't need a single. We'll just synch all the songs in the TV show, w make a big advertising thing about the album, and that'll be enough.'"

1. FOR PETE'S SAKE

One of the last songs recorded for *Headquarters*, Tork's "For Pete's Sake" lyrically presaged the rapidly approaching Summer of Love. The song, which was adopted as *The Monkees'* second-season closing theme, was cowritten by Tork's housemate, the late Joey Richards. Richards later cowrote The Byrds' single "Bad Night At The Whiskey" with Roger McGuinn.

Peter Tork: "The lyrics were just out of the air. It was really handy. It was just me playing these chords at my house, and Joey Richards threw in a couple of odds and ends of lines as I was going along. It just fell right into place. There was no particular reference; we weren't thinking about anything much. The lyrics sound a little silly to me now, but it was OK. Mike played the seventh changes on the organ. The thing about it that I remember is that one note is an added fourth; it's not a suspended. It was so weird, and it sounds so funky. I was really pleased with that. My first song on a Monkees record and my first song that I had written."

2. SUNNY GIRLFRIEND

This rollicking number was the first track taped specifically for the *Headquarters* album, on February 23, 1967. A brightly Nesmith country-rocker, the song was quickly adopted into The Monkees' live repertoire. It remained a fixture of the group's set list through their Far East tour in 1968. When the reunited foursome (clad in matching red velvet suits) performed it on their British *Justus* tour in 1997, it was hard to believe it wasn't 1967 all over again.

3. NO TIME

"No Time" grew out of a jam session with some "pro" players that took place toward the end of the *Headquarters* sessions. The results of that jam were haphazard and unusable, so a few days later the group (sans pros) returned to this simple 12-bar-style number on their own. This "group-only" recording was the most spirited performance on the entire album. With the quickly completed track at hand, a set of lyrics was composed to make light of their hectic schedule. Being that this was the last session for an already overdue album, they literally had "no time" to waste.

Michael Nesmith: "I think that was something that just popped up out of the session."

Micky Dolenz: "We were working real well together at that time. I remember we jus wanted to do a rock 'n' roll tune. I think that probably started off as a jam or maybe started off as 'Long Tall Sally.'"

Peter Tork: "'No Time' was just a Chuck Berry rip-off. Micky and Mike went out into the hall and wrote these weird-ass lyrics for it."

Micky Dolenz: "I remember Mike and I sitting in the control booth writing the lyric: Coming up with, 'Hober reeber sabasoben hobaseeba snick'—that was Bill Cosb who we were big fans of at the time. Then, 'Runnin' from the rising heat to find a plac to hide, the grass is always greener growing on the other side'—is police an marijuana. 'Andy, you're a dandy, you don't seem to make no sense'—is about And Warhol."[2]

When the song was completed, the writer's credit was given to engineer Hank Cical as a gift from the band.

Micky Dolenz: "We just gave him the song as a tip for being so loyal and such wonderful engineer for so many years. He made a lot of money off that! But we wro it; he didn't write it."

Peter Tork: "Hank got into a little trouble about it too, because engineers are no supposed to solicit songs. When RCA saw his name on the thing, they thought, 'Go he solicited this tune.' He had to go in there and explain."

Chip Douglas: "He was able to make a down payment on his first house with that. The were anxious to take care of everybody, because we'd all worked on it together an put in a lot of time and effort. It was a group effort definitely."

14. RANDY SCOUSE GIT

Headquarters' closing track is actually on of the first items recorded for the proje Written by Micky Dolenz in February 19 during a trip to London, the song w recorded a few days later.

Micky Dolenz: "It was the morning after Th Beatles had thrown us a party. I had son girl with me, and my friend was in the roc just sittin' around. I was literally making it u is I went along. It's not very significant, but it mentions The Beatles, it mentions this girl that I was with at the time, who later on was to become my first wife. She's the girl in the limousine. It was just about my experiences. It was like word association. Mama Cass is in there, The Monkees' experience of the limos and black, darkened windows and black leather Naugahyde. Then there was a social comment about being abused for having long hair. When I got back we were doing *Headquarters*, and I started playing it. I don't recall specifically how we managed to put the arrangement together, but it was a pretty collaborative effort at the time with Chip Douglas. I should think Chip had a lot to do with it."

Peter Tork: "God, I remember when Micky showed me that—I was so excited. (He) played me the verse, and he played me the chorus, and he said, 'And then at the end we do them both at the same time!' Wow, that was a brilliant piece of music. I've always thought that Micky was far more creative than he ever gave himself credit. I always thought that song was proof of it."

66-1007

The Monkees

COLGEMS.

PLEASANT VALLEY SUNDAY
WORDS

Printed in U.S.A.   ASK FOR THE MONKEES' LP ALBUMS

15. PLEASANT VALLEY SUNDAY (Single Version)

The Monkees hadn't had a single on the charts since "A Little Bit Me, A Little Bit You" in May, and "Pleasant Valley Sunday," recorded the day after the band's triumphant Hollywood Bowl concert, restored them to the Top 10 in July 1967. Written by the team of Goffin & King, "Pleasant Valley Sunday" is a social commentary on suburbia.

Chip Douglas: "It didn't take too many takes. Bill Chadwick played the rhythm guitar, and Mike played the lead live and then overdubbed it and fattened it up. That was my riff that I threw in there and taught to Mike. It took about two weeks for him to learn that. Not many guitar players can play the right way. I've seen them all try on the various stage bands—you know they don't quite have it right. It's kind of an offshoot of The Beatles song 'I Want To Tell You' but in different tempo and with different notes."

Michael Nesmith: "Chip came in and said, 'You know, what we need is a riff. We're living in the time of the riff: "Paperback Writer" and "Last Train To Clarksville," "Day Tripper." You know guitar riffs. How does this riff sound?' I said, 'Well, teach it to me. Let me see.' So he taught it to me, and he said, 'You know, we could put this to "Pleasant Valley Sunday," and it would really work well.' I said, 'That sounds good to me.' So I pulled out the Black Beauty (Nesmith's prized Gibson Les Paul model guitar), hooked up, and we made it. I remember that we went after the guitar sound. Everybody was

trying to get that great, big present guitar sound—nobody knew quite how to do it.
think I used three (Vox) Super Beatle (amplifiers) in the studio, playing really lou
trying to get the sound. It just ended up sounding like it does, kind of wooden. Ther
was a type of limiter/compressor called a UREI 1176, and boy, you could really suc
stuff out of the track. That was the first time that we really could do it. I think everybod
got a little carried away with the 1176 on that record."

Chip Douglas: "I wish I could hear the original demo, because there's a line in ther
that I can't recall if I got right. It's in the bridge, 'Creature comfort goals, can on
numb my soul and make it hard for me to see.' 'Make it hard for me to see,' for som
reason I had the impression that I didn't do the right line or changed it possibly.
remember seeing Carole King up at the Screen Gems office after we did "Pleasar
Valley Sunday." She kind of gave me this dirty look. I thought, 'Was it that line that I g
wrong perhaps, or didn't she like the guitar intro?'"[3]

The song's fade was a production innovation with the track feeding back into a
endless tunnel of reverb, finally crashing to a thunderous halt with the stopping of th
tape machine.

Chip Douglas: "We just did one take like that, and I think Hank said, 'How 'bout w
crank on some reverb and make this big psychedelic sort of ending.' I said, 'OK, fine
He just started to add the echo and boost the pre-echo, and that's they way it turne
out. We kept that take and thought, Wow, far out. Let's use this one."

Michael Nesmith: "That's just your standard psychedelic 'Whoa, let's leave th
on there!'"

Peter Tork: "It went into mush at the end. We let it fade off into echo and psycho-jell
We were pretty full of ourselves in those days, some of us anyway. Poor Davy nev
did get what this stuff was about."

16. WORDS
For the flip side of "Pleasant Valley Sunday," a Boyce & Hart song was rescued from th
More Of The Monkees sessions and recut. Using the old version as a model, the banc
new recording was almost identical, except for a moody organ solo from Peter Tor
which replaced the original version's flute piece. The final product was so strong th
it charted independently of "Pleasant Valley Sunday," at #11—the group's mc
successful B-side ever.

Bobby Hart: "'Words' was written before The Monkees project was given to us. It w
another one of the songs I was doing in the nightclubs with my band, The Candy Sto
Prophets. 'Words' and 'She' were from the same period of about six months. We we
highly influenced by the new psychedelic wave that was hitting L.A."

Tommy Boyce: "'Words' was a fabulous song. We had done *American Bandstand* way up in Bakersfield, and they had this hayride. There was this one girl kind of standing over to the side. So we said, 'Why don't you come on the hayride with us?' She said, 'No one really talks to me up here.' I said, 'Well, come on and have a great time.' Her name was Rosemarie. About two weeks later she sent us this unbelievable thank-you note. I remember I showed it to Bobby. As you opened the card, it just said in big letters 'WORDS can never express how nice you two were to me.' I said, 'Wow, what a great idea for a song—Words!' That's when we thought it would be a good idea to have Peter come in and sing with Micky. It's overlapping. Give him a chance to sing."

Chip Douglas: "I never really heard the other one very much, but it's something they wanted to do. We tried to do it as close to the original one, I guess. The only difference is there's Monkees in the background instead of Boyce & Hart."

17. DAYDREAM BELIEVER

John Stewart's "Daydream Believer" was the second-biggest-selling record of The Monkees' career and their fifth straight gold single. It is surprising then to note that "Daydream Believer" may have never been a hit if not for a bizarre twist of fate. The song "Love Is Only Sleeping" was

John Stewart

originally slated to follow "Pleasant Valley Sunday" as a single, but when the overseas masters did not arrive in time to make the scheduled simultaneous worldwide release, the single was postponed. Eleven days later Screen Gems officially scrapped the release, deciding that the more commercial flip side, "Daydream Believer," should be placed on the A-side. The revamped record was issued on October 25, 1967, and it became The Monkees' third and final chart-topping single a few weeks later. The song itself carries one small change from John Stewart's original. The line "Now you know how happy I can be" originally contained the word *funky* in place of *happy*. Some felt that Davy might sound awkward bragging about his funkiness, so this small change was made.[4]

18. GOIN' DOWN

The flip side of "Daydream Believer" was "Goin' Down," a group concoction that grew out of a spontaneous jam session. The chord progression was a spin-off of a Mose Allison blues alternately known as both "Parchman Farm Blues" and "Parchment Farm."

Michael Nesmith: "Peter had always loved to jam on 'Parchment Farm' and started off on this thing. We just headed off into la-la land. Then Micky started riffing this thing over the top of it."

Peter Tork: "Somebody gave me an arrangement of 'Parchman Farm' that a friend of theirs had sort of generated—the real folk process at work. I had played that version around for a while amongst the guys. I don't remember why we started playing it that day, but we just jammed it unrehearsed."

Micky Dolenz: "It was the exact same song, and we were covering it basically. So we did the tracks, and it came out real good. I remember Mike saying, 'All it is is the chord progression; we're not going to steal the melody or anything. Let's use this track but write other words, another melody to it. Why should we just cover somebody else's tune?' So I said, 'OK, fine. Good idea.'"

Peter Tork: "Next thing I knew Lester came to us and said, 'Listen, we've written some lyrics for that song, and we're gonna overdub some horns, and get Micky to go in and do it.' That was it. That was 'Goin' Down.' It was really great, you know, one of the things that can only come up if you're sort of engaged in the recordmaking process on a regular basis."

Micky Dolenz: "Diane Hilderbrand was given the track, and she was told to go away and write a song. She came back with this song, and I started practicing it. Singing it like this (adopts slow tempo). She said, 'No, no. It's twice that fast.' I was doing it half-time. I remember that I said, 'What?!' She said, 'Yes, it's twice that fast.' I get a lot of comments about that tune. (On the TV show) I did that live. You don't see nobody doing that stuff these days, do ya?"

19. SALESMAN

The Monkees' fourth album, *Pisces, Aquarius, Capricorn & Jones Ltd.*, put yet another spin on the group's sound. While they still played most of their own musical accompaniment, their recordings now featured a complement of sidemen to fill ou their sound. The album kicked off with "Salesman," a Nesmith twanger written by a protégé of Michael's named Craig Smith.

Michael Nesmith: "Craig Smith was a member of a band The Penny Arkade. It was Chris somebody and Craig, and they were writers and singers. I really liked the way they sang. I produced a couple of songs on 'em. They wrote one thing called 'Give Our Love To All The People,' which I just really liked. The reason I was drawn to 'Salesman' was because it reminded me of Sir Douglas and the Tex-Mex *oom-pah*."

Chip Douglas: "I used to see him around all the time. He was sometimes on the set and stuff. I saw him once when he was spaced out and had come back from Peru and had an album he was selling hand-to-hand. He had long hair and a spider tattooed in the middle of his forehead. He was just a nice kid, you know, a nice American boy. To see him years later was pretty bizarre. He said, 'Remember me? I used to be Craig Smith. My name is Maitreya Kali now.' He was pretty trippy."

Historical note: Craig Smith's (or Maitreya Kali's) homemade album *Apache* features his own version of "Salesman" with a lead vocal from none other than Mike Love of the Beach Boys! It is now a widely pirated psychedelic rarity.

20. THE DOOR INTO SUMMER

Unlike the publishing stalemate that occurred when the group tried to release Bill Martin's earlier "All Of Your Toys," no such conflict erupted over his "The Door Into Summer." This was the result of Martin's decision to move his songwriting interests to Screen Gems, which enabled him to freely submit material to the group. Despite Martin's optimism, this would be his sole released Monkees credit, though he would regularly contribute to future Monkees activities, group and solo. Of particular note, Martin was involved in a number of Michael Nesmith's video projects, including *Elephant Parts*, which in February 1982 won the first-ever Grammy® award for a video.

Bill Martin (songwriter): "The title was based on the Robert Heinlein book *The Door Into Summer*, which was about time travel. 'The Door Into Summer' is about the search for happiness and is basically an antiwar song."

Chip Douglas: "We did a demo of that together, Bill Martin and I. It had a real good feel to it, but we had to redo it for some reason. Someone didn't like it, one of the guys or something. I was always a little disappointed in the newer version from the original demo of it."

Bill Martin: "Micky tried singing it, and Mike tried it a couple of times also. The problem was that they didn't like the echo at RCA, so they strung a mike from Studio A to the men's bathroom. Mike did his vocal in there to achieve the right effect."

Michael Nesmith: "I didn't have anything to do with it. They said, 'Will you come sing?' That's all I did. I was not part of the creative process nor did I understand the process in any way. I was a hired singer."

21. LOVE IS ONLY SLEEPING

As previously noted, "Love Is Only Sleeping" was originally slated to be a single. When this did not come to pass, it became one of the many psychedelic-influenced songs on *Pisces, Aquarius, Capricorn & Jones Ltd.* The group first heard the song via a demo from songwriters Mann & Weil.

Michael Nesmith: "I remember when they would send me Barry and Cynthia's songs. We were always looking for songs to record. I just remember liking the song quite a bit in the demo."

Chip Douglas: "We all listened to the demos, and we all said, 'This one sounds good. Let's do this.' So it was group effort when it came to the demos; we'd all listen down. 'Love Is Only Sleeping' had a strange time signature to it: 7/4 time. I think (that riff) was on the original demo. It's a D tuning."

Peter Tork: "Kind of a smoky background, wasn't it? Kind of a little surreal. *Pisces, Aquarius* was all a mixed bag. I don't have any recollection of 'Love Is Only Sleeping.' I might not have been there."

22. CUDDLY TOY

Harry Nilsson's "Cuddly Toy" had been demoed specifically for The Monkees during a private session in March 1967. Nilsson had signed with RCA Records only a matter of weeks before and was just beginning to record his critically acclaimed *Pandemonium Shadow Show* album for the label. The Monkees cut the song in April 1967, making "Cuddly Toy" the oldest recording featured on *Pisces*, as well as the last Monkees studio recording to feature Micky on drums.

Harry Nilsson

Chip Douglas: "It might have been the first thing we did after *Headquarters*, because it was Micky on drums. It had the *Headquarters* sort of lineup on it."

Peter Tork: "That's me on piano. That I remember. There's something great about that one too. It was great to meet Harry. He was so talented and so obviously good right away."

Chip Douglas: "I'd known him from being with Phil Spector. He was still working at the bank when he was working for Spector. Never making any money."

Michael Nesmith: "Bill Martin brought Harry over while we were doing *Headquarters*. What I understood was that Harry was working at a bank at the time and writing songs on the side, trying to make a living at it. He had a stack of 'em, but I loved 'Cuddly Toy' when I heard it. I said, 'Oh man, we gotta do this.'"

23. WHAT AM I DOING HANGIN' 'ROUND?

Though it was originally credited to their '60s alter egos Travis Lewis and Boomer Clarke, "What Am I Doing Hangin' 'Round?" is actually the work of Michael Murphey

Michael Murphey and Owen Castleman

and Owen Castleman. The pseudonyms were part of the baggage of their incarnation as The Lewis & Clarke Expedition, who, along with Sajid Kahn and The New Establishment, made up the remainder of Colgems Records' non-Monkee artist roster.

Michael Nesmith: "I knew Michael from Dallas before The Monkees and had remained an acquaintance of his. Watched his songwriting. Thought of him as a good songwriter. One of the things that I felt was honest was country-rock. I wanted to move The Monkees more into that, because I felt like, 'Gee, if we get closer to country music, we'll get closer to blues, and country blues, and so forth.' Michael and Boomer Castleman—Boomer was his nickname—were writers at Screen Gems, and they wrote all kinds of really wonderful little songs, and 'Hangin' 'Round' was just one of them. I think Mike Murphey was more of the architect of that song than Boomer Castleman, but I don't know, they may have written it equally. It had a lot of uncountry' things in it: a familiar change from a I major to a 6th minor—those kinds of things. So it was kind of a new wave country song. It didn't sound like the country songs of the time, which was Buck Owens."

24. DAILY NIGHTLY

Michael Nesmith's "Daily Nightly" was a groundbreaking track for The Monkees. The lyrics were inspired by the November '66 riots on the Sunset Strip, while the music sounded like it came directly from outer space, via Micky Dolenz's use (the first-ever recorded on a pop record) of the Moog synthesizer.

Michael Nesmith: "I wrote it because I had bought a Hammond B-3. That guitar line—that's a keyboard lick that I'm not sure how it got over into the guitar, but it got over there. I may have done it or Chip may have done it. It was kind of a rambling comment on the Hollywood street scenes of the time. When Ben Frank's was going on and all that. As a matter of fact, somewhere around that time (the nightclub) Pandora's Box had burned down. Pandora's Box was at the intersection of Crescent Heights and (Sunset Boulevard). That was a very important corner there, and they had caught a bus on fire, which had then in turn burned down Pandora's Box. That was the first real time that those crazy kids got out of control. I was amused by the obvious inability of the press to digest this information; they just didn't have any sense of what was going on at all. Completely lost. So I just wrote it down in that poem."

Micky Dolenz: "That was the first time anybody had used a Moog as far as I know on a pop album. I had the first Moog on the West Coast. Somebody introduced me to this guy in L.A. named Paul Beaver; he was representing the Moog Company out here. I went over to his workshop and saw one in operation. I was blown away and ordered one immediately to go on the road—it was built in traveling cases. We took it on the road—it was kind of weird—hell of a thing to set up. It was a monstrosity to operate compared to what's around now. It was very difficult to tune. So, Paul Beaver came around and helped me set it up and tune it. It was pretty exciting. I remember Mike was really into it. He thought it was incredible, because it was state of the art at the time."

25. STAR COLLECTOR

Goffin & King's "Star Collector" closed the *Pisces, Aquarius, Capricorn & Jones Ltd.* album with more spacey Moog music—and a somewhat salacious lyric for The Monkees. The song, which dealt with the growing phenomena of rock groupies, predated The Rolling Stones' similarly themed (and titled) "Star Star" by some six years. Also of note, a Moog "professional," the late Paul Beaver, was brought in to twiddle the knobs and handle the more musically complex parts on "Star Collector."

Chip Douglas: "After Micky experimented with his synthesizer I thought, 'Well, let's find a real synthesizer player.' I'd heard about Paul Beaver; Micky had told me about him. He was a good player, and he knew what to do."

Peter Tork: "Micky's Moog part on 'Daily Nightly' was, I thought, brilliant. Another example of his intense creativity when he was into it. He just made the Moog stand up and speak in a way that Paul Beaver didn't. It was like Paul thought it was a flute or something. He was kind of out there musically, but it was still within the normal harmonic bounds. Micky just went out there with this stuff; it was about screeches and swoops. I went to a party at Micky's house once with a friend, and we were standing there, and I said, 'And there is the famous Moog synthesizer. Micky's one of the better

Moog players around.' Micky came by at that moment, and he said, 'Yeah, but it's even better if it plays itself.' He pushed a few knobs and turned the thing on and then walked away. It honked and did things on an absolutely random basis, never repeated itself. It was so interesting. You know he was really out there, Dolenz. One of my great regrets is that he wasn't able to credit himself for his own creativity. That to me is one of the great tragedies of the history of The Monkees. Maybe the greatest single tragedy, aesthetically anyway."

Disc 3 1968 1. VALLERI

After two albums, a hectic summer tour, and a busy shooting schedule for their second series, The Monkees began to pursue their recording activities separately. Ironically, these individually produced and recorded tracks all bore the same collective credit: "Produced by The Monkees." In reality, the first release made under this pact was not produced by a Monkee and, in fact, only featured one Monkee on it (Davy Jones). Instead this single saw the return of Boyce & Hart, who reluctantly ventured back into the studio to recut the year-old "Valleri." "Valleri" became The Monkees' last Top 10 single and final gold record.

Bobby Hart: "Lester Sill came back to us and said, 'They want you to recut "Valleri," but we can't use the original track because the musicians union contracts were filed with you as producers, and you can't have producer's credit. We want you to go back in and do it again, making it sound as close to the original as possible and not take producer's credit on it.' So, that's what we did."

TAPIOCA TUNDRA

Michael Nesmith's "Tapioca Tundra" was, hands down, the strangest Monkees Top 40 hit. As the charting flip side of "Valleri," it speaks volumes about the band's popularity that this off-kilter record soared as high as #34 on the Pop chart. A musical meeting of "Winchester Cathedral"-like nostalgia coupled with lyrics that were just pure whimsy, the song sounds like a jam session with Tito Puente and The New Vaudeville Band.

Michael Nesmith: "I wonder if 'Tapioca Tundra' and 'Daily Nightly' came out of the same thing? I have always enjoyed writing poetry. Stand-alone poetry. As a matter of fact, one of the ways I got into songwriting was to find poems and see if I could put them to music. I did that in high school and college. In English class I would set some of these poems we were studying to music. It was from there that I decided that I would enjoy writing poetry. About the time that 'Tapioca Tundra' and 'Daily Nightly' came along, I had been writing my own poetry for a while. I realized that I couldn't continue to write pop tunes of the type that Neil Diamond, Goffin, King, and Boyce & Hart were writing. I just thought I probably ought to go ahead and put my own imprimatur on things and write those songs. They had actually been poems that I had been writing for a long time on my own. If they tend to be metaphorical and they tend to be more imaginative and complex, that was from poetry I was writing. They weren't really designed as songs at all."

3. DREAM WORLD

Davy Jones' "Dream World" kicked off The Monkees' fifth album, *The Birds, The Bees & The Monkees*. The song was a collaboration with Steve Pitts and hearkens back to Jones' first recording sessions in early 1965.

Davy Jones: "Steve Pitts was a musician from Austin who was a friend of Mike Nesmith's. During the course of *The Monkees*' filming Mike introduced a lot of people to us. Steve Pitts and I sat down to write some tunes originally for the movie *Head*. We also had written some other tunes during that particular session. The idea of 'Dream World' was a bit of a cop-out—or a bit of a steal in a sense, not the song itself, but the idea. I'd done a thing years before with Colpix Records, a song called 'Dream Girl.' I wanted to try to incorporate some of the violins and all that early-'60s stuff on it. We were very restricted to our studio time and budget availability. Prior to that it had been Tommy Boyce, Bobby Hart, Jeff Barry, and all the other people who had carte blanche with our money. That was like our first try at going in and being a producer, which I would rarely attempt now. It's a really specialized thing, producing."

4. AUNTIE'S MUNICIPAL COURT

"Auntie's Municipal Court" is probably Nesmith's most accessible offering included on *The Birds, The Bees & The Monkees*. The song grew out of a studio jam in which Nesmith coupled one of his poems with some of guitar player Keith Allison's improvised riffs. Allison, best known as a latter-day member of Paul Revere & The Raiders, was another pre-Monkees buddy of Nesmith's from Texas and had also notably appeared on some of Boyce & Hart's early Monkees productions. Keith later toured with Dolenz, Jones, Boyce & Hart.

5. P.O. BOX 9847

Cut alongside the remake of "Valleri," Boyce & Hart's "P.O. Box 9847" had previously been a solo single for the duo (albeit a B-side). While the song's arrangement remained almost identical, the main difference between releases was that Boyce & Hart's solo single credited Monkees creator Bob Rafelson as cowriter of the song.

Bobby Hart: "It was Bob Rafelson's idea to do a song about a classified ad. He said have a great idea for a song worded the way a classified ad would be in the abbreviated style.' So we wrote 'P.O. Box 9847' and gave him a third of the song for his inspiration and original idea. The powers that be would not let him have a writer's credit. I don't know why. I guess it was some sort of conflict of interest being producer on the show. He never cashed his first royalty check, and they took his name off subsequently."

ZOR AND ZAM

Bill and John's Chadwick "Zor And Zam" brought *The Birds, The Bees & The Monkees* album to an epochal close. The song features a thunderous arrangement from Shorty Rogers, and the lyrics finally gave the group an overt antiwar anthem. Sung and predominately produced by Micky Dolenz, "Zor And Zam" was also featured in the final episode of The Monkees.

Micky Dolenz: "'Zor And Zam' was a great tune. I remember hearing Bill Chadwick singing it at a party. We used to hang out. He was one of the sidekick/bodyguards/stand-ins. I said, 'God, wow, man I'd really like to do that song.' So we brought it in, and we did it."

Bill Chadwick (songwriter): "Originally my brother and I had written a treatment for a television series called *The Friendship*. He was a former Disney animator, and it was to (have combined) live action and animation. It was (a) very fantasy-oriented (story about) some guys sailing on a ship, and the ship went into a whirlpool. If you can imagine *Yellow Submarine* with live action and about three or fours years earlier, that's what the concept was. 'Zor And Zam' was one of the songs in the pilot. We never did anything with it. We got bogged down in the creative end. I got involved with The Monkees and

Bobby Hart, Keith Allison & Tommy Boyce

used the song there. It was about two kings that gave a war, and nobody came. We all had friends going off to Vietnam and nobody was happy about the way thing were being handled. Guys were going over there and weren't getting any support you're not going to get support from your own country, why the hell should you go

7. CARLISLE WHEELING (First Recorded Version)

Michael Nesmith's "Carlisle Wheeling" was an outtake from *The Birds, The Bees & The Monkees* sessions with a tortured history. At least three versions of the song were c between 1967 and 1968, yet none of them were deemed worthy of release. During I solo sessions of the early '70s, Nesmith rerecorded the song under the tit "Conversations," but even this take did not satisfy the author.

Michael Nesmith: "I had tried several times (and) the problem was not in th recording; the problem was in the song. Early in life as an artist, and certainly befo The Monkees ever came along, I was casting about for native design keys—*nati* meaning native to myself—that I could work in. One of the ones that was mo satisfying and very easy for me was delight. Another one was whimsy, and they ha served me well as I have gotten more and more into them. The problem is, when yo work in delight and whimsy, you are beset on all sides. It is a razor-edge line to wa and the foment is poignancy, sentimentality, maudlin, and all of the things that ta those dandy little notions and just cast them into the worst elements of sentimental and shallowness. I'm afraid that as I was making an attempt to write th 'Conversations' song, I got knocked off the straight and narrow. This was a song reverie, and it was a song of retrospection and contemplation. Those dynamics c just as subject to poignancy and sentimentality as anything else. That's wh happened to this song, it just got cratered. I started to torture the metaphors ar torture the similes. 'The phoenix of our love'— I mean, please. We're just right off ir 'Excuse-me land.' All of us have got to do one of those, I suppose. 'So forgive me r dear if I seem preoccupied.' I know that we're both old and settled in now, and v don't say much to each other, but that doesn't mean that I still don't love you. No that's a nice, sweet dynamic for a song. Unfortunately, I managed to murder pretty good."[5]

8. TEAR THE TOP RIGHT OFF MY HEAD

Despite the fact that he was the first Monkee to break away and do his own thing in t studio, Peter Tork had the greatest trouble getting his songs accepted and completi his productions. Countless takes of his "Lady's Baby" and "The Merry Go Round Son were made at dozens of sessions, but very few of his recordings were ever tr completed. Tork soldiered on regardless, cutting beautiful songs with members of T Buffalo Springfield and future Jimi Hendrix sideman Buddy Miles. One of his best from t era, "Tear The Top Right Off My Head" existed in numerous takes (including some w Micky on vocals). Unfortunately, most of these tapes have long since disappeared, ar we are archivally left with only a thumbnail sketch of what Tork was up to at that tin

The song's title was derived from a popular expression among Tork's friends.

Peter Tork: "It was an expression of how radical the feelings could get. Obviously you know the expression *dynamite*: 'Boy, it was dynamite,' meaning it was great. Everybody tries to top the last one. 'Boy, she really affected me. Boy, she ripped my arms off.' It was sort of au courrant at the time. It wasn't exactly the most common expression, you know, but it really was on the street. It worked around the chord changes. The whole structure seemed to be in two parts. There was this kind of quiet, normal, everyday pedestrian feel, and that was the first section. Then (in) the blues section things are frying, the ends of your hair are sizzling, because something radical is happening here. That was all the song was about."

9. THE GIRL I LEFT BEHIND ME (First Recorded Version)

Neil Sedaka and Carole Bayer's "The Girl I Left Behind Me" had been tried at the end of the *More Of The Monkees* sessions but was held by Kirshner for a future release. The Monkees eventually got back to the song (or at least Davy Jones did) with a new take cut in late 1967. For some unknown reason this new recording was held from release, too, and the production of this tune struggled on through more rerecordings. Ultimately, a 1968 take found its way onto The Monkees seventh album, *Instant Replay*, in February 1969. This box set contains the less common, but clearly superior, take from 1967.

Neil Sedaka: "There is a phrase I've come to hate over the years: 'If not this album, the next album.' I'll explain that. Don Kirshner heard 'When Love Comes Knockin' (At Your Door)' and 'The Girl I Left Behind,' and he said, 'Well, we're going to put "When Love Comes Knockin' (At Your Door)" on the album, but we'll reserve "The Girl I Left Behind Me" for the next album. That has stuck with me through the years. I was so discouraged because it was left off the album. As a result I lost a lot of money."

10. NINE TIMES BLUE

Michael Nesmith's "Nine Times Blue" had been demoed as early as 1967's *Headquarters* sessions, but it was not until the following year that he would get serious about recording a master version. He had initially tried the song with full band including drums before later settling on the simpler guitar, bass, and vocal take included here. Historically, this track marks the first recorded work of Red Rhodes (the late pedal steel virtuoso) with Michael Nesmith. Rhodes would go on to play an integral musical role in Nesmith's solo career.

Historical note: In July 1969 The Monkees made a guest appearance on *The Johnny Cash Show*. Their segment included a live rendition of "Nine Times Blue," which was introduced as a "song from our album." As it turned out, "Nines Time Blue" never appeared on a Monkees album at the time and was not released until 1987's *Missing Links*.

11. COME ON IN

Peter Tork produced this version of folk singer/songwriter Jo Mapes' "Come On In"
during early 1968. The song has the aural quality of a Buffalo Springfield recording,
and it was no doubt captured at an offshoot session with members of the band.

Although Tork produced songs of obvious quality, he was
not represented at all on *The Birds, The Bees & The Monkees*
album. This track eventually appeared on *Missing Links
Volume Two*.

Davy Jones: "There's one song that Peter Tork sings on the
Missing Links album where he sounds absolutely super. He's
right on the button, and he wasn't supposed to be a singer.
The other guys were always pushing him out. He was being
downtrodden by the studio in regards to his recording, his
playing, his songs, and everything else. The guy was the salt
of the earth, Peter Tork. It wasn't just Hare Krishna,
waterbeds, and brown rice. That guy was a very, very
accomplished musician."

12. D.W. WASHBURN

Leiber & Stoller's "D.W. Washburn" was The Monkees' seventh single release and final
Top 40 chart placement of the '60s. The song was suggested by Lester Sill and
sounded not unlike a Coasters outtake from the '50s. Ironically, The Coasters rushed
out their own version in an attempt to beat The Monkees' record to the punch. Neither
version was destined to succeed commercially because the song was hopelessly out
of step with the times.

Lester Sill: "I loved the sound of the song—the demo that I heard. Then I realized after
we did it and it came out that it was really a downer. It was a story about a guy in the
gutter, about a bum. I thought that there was kind of a comical, Dixieland feel to it
that I felt was rather different. In hindsight, I
realized it was an awful mistake."

Peter Tork: "Boy! Originally there was a
black bass singer on the take. Bert said,
'Wait a minute. It's one thing to have
Tommy and Bobby singing 'ohhs' and
'ahhs' in the background; it's another to
have a prominent black bass singer
responding that way.' The only thing about
that song that was notable is that it's Leiber-
Stoller. I imagine it was an old Leiber-Stoller

Jerry Leiber & Mike Stoller

tune from way, way back that nobody had done yet. It sounds like middle Coasters, you know. The thing about The Monkees project at the end was, I think basically Bert and Bob were running out of steam. That's what I think. I think for some reason, somehow, they had had it. They started off with a lot of enthusiasm, and I think the pressures brought them down. I think Bert's still reeling, to tell you the truth."

13. IT'S NICE TO BE WITH YOU

"It's Nice To Be With You" was the flip side of "D.W. Washburn," and it tread on more familiar territory musically. The song showed a respectable placing in the U.S. charts (#51), and in the Philippines (where other Davy Jones-sung songs like "Hard To Believe" and "We Were Made For Each Other" charted high) the song actually reached #1. The song's author, Jerry Goldstein, is a legendary writer, producer, and onetime member of the studio group The Strangeloves.

14. ST. MATTHEW

n June 1968 Michael Nesmith took a trip to Nashville to fish and record. The recordngs that he produced were another step in his pioneering journey as an architect of country-rock. The song "St. Matthew" is actually better defined as cosmic country-rock, since it features an obscure set of lyrics filtered through the whirling effect of a Leslie speaker cabinet. The song was inspired by Bob Dylan, whose own country-rock blend on the album *Nashville Skyline* was only months away.

Michael Nesmith: "The lyrics had been a poem that were laying around for a long ime. I had given (them) to a stack of different songwriters to see if they could write a melody. The track just came out of a foolin'-around session with the band n Nashville. Another attempt to marry country and rock. It's a song about Bob Dylan. The 'steal and kneel' is a reference

Mike Nesmith with Nashville musicians

to 'She Belongs To Me.' 'She will start out standing, proudly steal her anything she needs. You will wind up peeking through a keyhole down upon your knees.' The *she* in that is the 'St. Matthew' that I'm referring to, and the 'St. Matthew' that I'm referring to is biblical. It refers to the biblical sense of the Holy Ghost as the central character in 'She Belongs To Me.' As I think about that song many times, and I have many times, I realize that it was prescient to his 'born again' phase. 'Cause I could see that what he was doing was wandering into the areas of biblical representations of the Holy Ghost, and I was convinced at the time that he did not know that he was doing that. It was interesting to me, so that was what the song was about. But, you know, that's so totally obscure that I didn't ever expect anybody to understand it or try and communicate anything with it. It was just a song, a little note that I wrote to myself in a way."[6]

15. PORPOISE SONG (Theme From *Head*) (Single Version)

The mesmerizing "Porpoise Song" opened The Monkees' movie, *Head*, in a psychedelic swirl of sound. The song (subtitled "From 'Head'—A New Motion Picture") was written specifically for the project by songwriters Goffin & King, who perhaps also had Micky Dolenz in mind to sing the lead vocal.

Micky Dolenz: "I was told that by somebody. If you listen to it, it's about me committing suicide. It was written for the movie. It wasn't a song that she pulled out of a drawer. 'Riding the backs of giraffes for laughs,' I'm sure, was a reference to *Circus Boy*. At least I was told that."

Peter Tork: "I wouldn't know a thing about it. They made a decision to release the 'Porpoise Song' from the album for the movie. I think it was premature. If they had released any of the others (first), then the 'Porpoise Song' would have been a good one to come back with. In retrospect you can tell it wasn't right."

16. AS WE GO ALONG

Carole King and Toni Stern's "As We Go Along" provided a mellow acoustic counterpoint to the lush psychedelia of "Porpoise Song." The single release of "Porpoise Song" was a major chart disappointment, and its B-side, "As We Go Along," received only minor airplay at the time, bubbling under the Hot 100 at #106.

Micky Dolenz: "That was a bitch to sing. It was in 5/4 time or some bizarre signature. I had a lot of trouble picking it up. Typically, we didn't have a lot of time to rehearse this stuff. We were filming. I'd go in, and they'd play the song a few times. I remember that was a tough song to sing, but I loved it. I still love it. It's actually one of my favorites."

Peter Tork: "Carole King is an astounding creature. The 'Porpoise Song' is a great song, and I think 'As We Go Along' is even better. Carole King could write with anybody. She could write with Mike Nesmith, after all!"

17. DITTY DIEGO-WAR CHANT

Although "Porpoise Song" was labeled as the film's theme song, *Head*'s anthem was surely the "Ditty Diego-War Chant." Recorded under the title "Movie Jingle," this short satirical rewrite of "Theme From The Monkees" was penned by Jack Nicholson and Bob Rafelson. With lyrics about the group's "manufactured image," the recitation captured the real-life subplot of *Head*, which was to destroy The Monkees' career as teen idols. According to Nicholson biographer Patrick McGilligan, these destructive ploys were not restricted to the film's sardonic script and jingle. During production on *Head*, Bob Rafelson would attempt to dispirit group members via a subtle campaign of derision. McGilligan notes, ". . . the director would put on an LP by more high voltage rockers, the Electric Flag or Neil Young, and bait (Davy) Jones with the comment, 'That's real rock 'n' roll, man!'"

With Jack Nicholson

18. CIRCLE SKY (Live)

Despite the producers' efforts to divide the group, *Head* contained the band's most assertive performance as a unit on Michael Nesmith's "Circle Sky." A fierce rocker, the film featured a live version of the song from a May 1968 performance in Salt Lake City.

Michael Nesmith: "'Circle Sky' was a song that I wrote while I was in the band with The Monkees, thinking of what would be a good, simple, aggressive rock 'n' roll tune. It was written around the concept of the band playing as a band. A good example of it is 'Hamilton smiling down,' (which) refers to the name on the music stand that I was sitting in front of. They were made-up lyrics to represent a collage of the times of The Monkees playing as a band. It's one of the reasons it's one of the best things that The Monkees do as a band. Very simple, straight-ahead, power-trio stuff."

Although the film itself contained this electrifying performance in full, the original soundtrack album substituted a less invigorating studio cut produced by Nesmith without the rest of the group in late 1967.

Michael Nesmith: "I don't have any idea how that happened. I think that The Monkee always played it better. I can't remember a studio version being better than the wa we played it live. 'Cause live it was just pure unbridled energy."

Historical note: The band later recut the song "Circle Sky" with some slightly altere lyrics for their 1997 *Justus* album.

19. CAN YOU DIG IT

Peter Tork made his most significant musical showing on a Monkees album with th *Head* soundtrack. The first of Tork's two songs from the set was "Can You Dig It." Th song was inspired by his study of the Tao Te Ching and was originally recorded wit Peter handling all the vocals. When the song became part of the movie soundtrac Micky took over as lead singer.

Peter Tork: "It was Bert's (decision to have Micky sing lead) because it fell into the scheme they had for the song in the movie. It's right after Micky's desert scene. The first song Mike ever produced had Micky because Micky was the lead singer. Neither Mike then, nor I later, thought twice about it. Later on we thought, 'We should do this ourselves because it's our song.' We didn't have any of that proprietary interest until afterwards. 'Can You Dig It' is about the Tao. The hook line I wrote in my dressing room on the set. The chords for the chorus I'd written in college and had just stuck with me. I hadn't been able to do a thing with them until I was sittin' writing on a scrap of paper with ideas, and I wrote, 'Can you dig it/Do you know/Would you like to let it show.' Those three as a triplet—as opposed to a couplet. I just looked at them and (went), 'Wow!' I grabbed a pencil and circled those three. They were part of a quatrain. I said, 'Wait a minute—no, this works best as a little three-line thing chorus there.' I was very happy with myself."[7]

20. DADDY'S SONG
(Previously Unissued Long Version)

Davy Jones' showpiece in *Head* is Harry Nilsson's "Daddy's Song." Lyrically, the song recalls Nilsson's earlier "1941" (which had also been demoed for the group in March 1967). Musically, the song is similar in style to "Cuddly Toy" and replaced an almost identical song by Bill Chadwick called "If You Have The Time." Although "Daddy's Song" was undoubtedly molded to suit Jones' "Broadway rock" style, it was originally cut by Nesmith.

Peter Tork: "'Daddy's Song' I thought was great. I loved Harry Nilsson's work; he did great stuff for us. I was awfully sorry to hear him go."

Historical note: Nilsson recorded his own version of "Daddy's Song" for his RCA album *Ariel Ballet*. However, the chances were so strong that "Daddy's Song" would be a Monkees single that RCA (who manufactured and distributed The Monkees records) promptly deleted the song from Nilsson's album. As it it turned out, no single of the song was forthcoming in this country, although Great Britain did issue the track as a single in place of "Porpoise Song."

21. LONG TITLE: DO I HAVE TO DO THIS ALL OVER AGAIN

Tork's "Long Title: Do I Have To Do This All Over Again" was at one time part of *The Birds, The Bees & The Monkees* album. However, this album went through a selection shake-up for reasons unknown, and Tork's two cuts (the other being a spoken work piece called "Alvin") were completely dropped. When issued in remixed form on

Head, the song became Peter's last release with The Monkees. Tork left the group afte[r] taping the television special *33 1/3 Revolutions Per Monkee* in late 1968.

Peter Tork: "Rafelson heard an acetate of all those tunes: 'Can You Dig It,' 'Lon[g] Title,''Lady's Baby,' and I think a couple of others. (He) picked those two for *Head* o[ut] of the blue. I didn't even think about the movie particularly. I remember very well th[at] the song just fell out of me one day. I was just playing those chord changes on th[e] guitar and opened my mouth, and that's what popped out. Once I had the first vers[e,] the second verse followed the theme for the first verse. The weird thing is that the son[g] has been prophetic. I had no idea that that was going to be my attitude about an[y]thing having to do with music when I wrote the song. It just came out that way. I wro[te] the lyric in London."

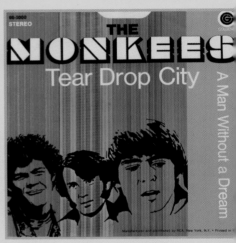

Disc 4 1969-96

1. TEAR DROP CITY

After the departure of Tork and the commercial failure of *Head*, The Monkees returned to the public eye with a song that recalled their first hit, "Last Train To Clarksville." The song was an older recording from 1966 that was remixed and significantly sped up for release. In the end the single only boosted the group's fortunes slightly, reaching a middling #56 on the Pop chart in February 1969.

Tommy Boyce: "That was the last Monkees hit, and it was one of the last songs we wro[te] for The Monkees. I always thought that should have been more popular than it was, b[ut] the group were split up by then. In fact, we also did it on a Boyce & Hart album. W[e] wrote that one day in a park. We were walking down Lankershim Boulevard of [all] places. We just sat down on a bench with the guitar and started playing this riff. I thi[nk] it was sort of like the riff to 'She's About A Mover.'"

Bobby Hart: "We were just experimenting along the lines of the seventh chord aga[in,] which The Beatles had used in several songs. We thought there was maybe room [for] another song besides 'Clarksville' using that seventh kind of progression. They told u[s it] was going to be a single, but it wasn't our decision. Things started changing after Pe[ter] quit. They were putting out things that were already in the can."

2. A MAN WITHOUT A DREAM

Goffin & King's "A Man Without A Dream" was featured on the flip side of "Tear Dr[op] City." The song marked the debut of Bones Howe as the group's producer. Howe h[ad] previously engineered and produced such groups as The Turtles, The Mamas & T[he] Papas, The Association, and The 5th Dimension. Despite his hitmaking history, t[he] roup's relationship with Howe was relatively short-lived. After producing two single ides and the songs for their television special *33 1/3 Revolutions Per Monkee*, no urther Howe productions were cut.

ones Howe (producer): "What happened was all the guys were making records on heir own, and they were looking for somebody to produce Davy. So I did those two acks with Davy: 'Man Without A Dream' and 'Someday Man.' I had a lot of records on he charts so that probably had something to do with it. I went about it the same way went about everything that I did at that time, which was looking for the best song for he artists I was working with."

avy Jones: "There was one guy I recorded with. I did a song called 'A Man Without A ream': 'With the music of life my soul is out of tune,' down in the range that I was upposed to be singing in—not where they had me singing all the time. I'm a baritone, nd I always have been. I don't understand why we were given so little thought and onsideration along the line."[8]

THROUGH THE LOOKING GLASS

he band's seventh album, *Instant Replay*, was a grab bag of tracks from various ses- ons dating between October 1966 and January 1969. One of the best songs includ- d is Boyce & Hart's "Through The Looking Glass." The song had been recorded for *ore Of The Monkees* then later recut for *The Birds, The Bees & The Monkees*. After being umped off both those albums, the song finally landed on *Instant Replay*, which was sued on February 15, 1969.

mmy Boyce: "Boy, I always liked that song. We always thought it should have been single, but it kept getting pushed aside. We decided one day to put horns on it, then e knew it should have been a single. It was an imaginary song we wrote about a ouple of girls we knew. Sort of like an *Alice In Wonderland*-type of thing, you walk rough the mirror—'Through The Looking Glass,' going through this glass into a fferent world."

obby Hart: "I don't know if this was after The Jefferson Airplane song "White Rabbit." ems like it has almost the same kind of idea of using *Alice In Wonderland*. A sychedelic analogy."

I WON'T BE THE SAME WITHOUT HER

ichael Nesmith's production of "I Won't Be The Same Without Her" was yet another pe-vault nugget exhumed on *Instant Replay*. This Goffin & King song was originally it at the July 1966 session for "Sweet Young Thing" and was another product of their fated partnership with Nesmith. Coincidentally, "I Won't Be The Same Without Her" so utilized the same high-hat pattern that was the trademark of Nesmith's "You Just ay Be The One." An early version of that song was also cut during this session.

5. YOU AND I

One of the few fresh recordings on *Instant Replay*, "You And I" is a standout f
several reasons. The song features some searing guitar work from Neil Young, while
lyrics aptly summed up The Monkees' precarious commercial fortunes. The song w
a collaboration between Davy Jones and Bill Chadwick.

Davy Jones: "It was just the old story. All of a sudden we were being pushed under th
mat because *The Partridge Family* and that crew were coming along. We were ju
about to be moved aside, and they were gonna go and spend their mone
somewhere else. It's such an unbelievably tragic shame, you know. I'm sure the
would have wished in the early '70s we would have croaked, and now we'd be fo
heroes. It didn't work out that way. We're all still working."

Bill Chadwick: "I originally wrote the lyrics. It was kind of a poem to a friend. We we
both moving up in the entertainment business and realized that it's not a lasting thin
to say the least. One day you're at the top, and the next day you're at the bottor
That's what it was about. Davy (and I) edited some of the lyrics together and create
the melody and arrangement. Davy was always great to work with because h
wouldn't work with somebody unless he had a lot of respect for them."

6. WHILE I CRY

Michael Nesmith's solemn "While I Cry" is another of *Instant Replay*'s highlights. Th
track was recorded over two sessions at RCA Victor Studio in Hollywood in early 19
for *The Birds, The Bees & The Monkees*. Although it was mixed alongside his other tun

r that album, it is disputable as to whether "While I Cry" was really intended for the
pril 1968 long-player. In early 1969, the song was remixed and sweetened by Nesmith
nd engineer Pete Abbott for release on *Instant Replay*.

ichael Nesmith: "Geez, I did that for The Monkees? For some reason I did not remem-
er that as a Monkees song. It has kind of a rolling guitar intro. That's me playing
uitar. That was a guitar lick that I was just foolin' around with and wrote a song around
e lick. Not an uncommon move."

SHORTY BLACKWELL

icky Dolenz's grand production piece "Shorty Blackwell" grew out of a lyrical word-
ay about his pet cat of the same name. Reportedly, the other cryptic lyric lines refer
 an unspecified member of the group ("He built a house upon a hill") and the actu-
 process of recordmaking ("Black and shiny, now you finally gotten everything you
anted, and you're taunted by the power that you really don't want anymore; every-
ody's talking faster, hurry up, get me a master"). The song's mammoth orchestral
rangement was provided by another Shorty—famed jazz trumpeter and arranger,
e late Shorty Rogers.

Micky Dolenz: "I liked Shorty Rogers. We had a great time working together. That w
my little attempt to do 'A Day In The Life' or something. Just me again being incredib
self-indulgent and writing about things that were happening in my life. Sho
Blackwell was my cat. My feeble attempt at something to do with *Sgt. Pepper*."[9]

8. IF I EVER GET TO SAGINAW AGAIN

An altogether more straightforward version of Nesmith's country-rock was apparent
"If I Ever Get To Saginaw Again." The song was cowritten by Jack Keller, who ha
previously produced and wrote songs for the band's early albums. Nesmith's versi
of this song was never originally released, and Keller later brought the song to Da
Jones, who produced an additional unreleased version in the 1970s.

9. SMILE

Davy Jones' mellow "Smile" was recorded in May 1968 alongside his Bill Chadwi
collaboration "You And I." Chadwick and Jones produced this session together, whi
included a stellar crew of musicians.

Bill Chadwick: "Hal Blaine played drums, Max Bennett played bass, and Neil You
played lead guitar. He was a personal friend of mine, and I wanted to hear his gui
sound. I asked a couple of other people to try and play it, and I started thinking, *W*
the hell would I have somebody else play Neil's sound when I can call Neil? So I d
That was the first session that Hal Blaine used roto-toms on. In fact, when he walkec
he said, 'Wow, they're here!'"

10. LISTEN TO THE BAND (Single Version)

The Monkees' new "big band sound" (as carried forth on their tour with Sam & T
Goodtimers) was highlighted on the April 1969 single "Listen To The Band." An inter
horn-driven country rocker, the single was not the tremendous success that was hope
but it still stands as one of The Monkees' last great stabs at creativity. The son
anthem-like lyrics are often construed as a commentary on The Monkees' musi
plight, though Nesmith considers "Listen To The Band" to be more of an experimen
musical style and sensibility.

Michael Nesmith: "'Listen To The Band' was the architecture for country-rock. . . . I gues
was the same embryo beating in me that was somewhere in Don Henley, Glenn Fr
Linda Ronstadt, and Neil Young—everybody who was hanging out in those times. I co
just feel this happening, that there was this *thing*. So, I headed off to Nashville to see
couldn't get some of the Nashville country thing into rock 'n' roll or vice versa. What I fou
out was that Nashville country was not the country that was going to be the basis
country-rock. It was coming much more out of the Southern California scene. So I enc
up with a lot of Dobro, mandolin, and banjo and things which were hard-core mount
music stuff that didn't really work, although 'Listen To The Band' worked pretty good."

11. SOMEDAY MAN

Recorded at the same sessions as "A Man Without A Dream," Paul Williams and Roger Nichols' "Someday Man" became Bones Howe's second and final released production for The Monkees. As a single it reached a disappointing #81 on the Pop chart in May 1969. The song is mainly notable for being the first non-Screen Gems copyright the group were allowed to release.

Bones Howe: "They had always recorded songs either from Screen Gems, or they recorded their own material. We were able to convince Colgems that we could do an outside song. I guess it was because we looked around, and I kept saying to them, 'Find me another song that'll knock this one out of the box.' No one could find a song that everybody liked better."

Paul Williams

Davy Jones: "I went to them many, many times with Paul Williams' tunes. Not because Three Dog Night were doing them and not because anybody else was doing them. They were just great tunes, but they felt they were too sophisticated. It was a bit complicated for The Monkees at the time. Unfortunately, it never even got a showing. I like the tune. I like Paul Williams. I thought Bones Howe was a bit busy."

12. SOME OF SHELLY'S BLUES

This version of Michael Nesmith's "Some Of Shelly's Blues" is another gem from his mid-'68 Nashville sessions. The song is probably best known for its cover versions from Linda Ronstadt's Stone Poneys, The Nitty Gritty Dirt Band, and a '70s Nesmith solo version. Despite the song's strong country bent, it was actually written in the early '60s when he was a struggling folkie.

Roger Nichols

Michael Nesmith: "That was out of the 'Different Drum' period, when I was playing with a guitar and harmonica."

13. MOMMY AND DADDY

While Nesmith was exploring the greate realms of roots music, Micky Dolenz found c creative voice in reality-based songwriting Set to a "Randy Scouse Git"-like backing track, "Mommy And Daddy" is an astonish ing list of questions that he wanted hi preteen audience to ask their parents Touching on the plight of Native American and the hypocrisy of prescription drug use the song was without equal for its shoc

value alone. Despite its controversial and confrontational lyrics, "Mommy And Daddy" still managed to attract sporadic regional airplay. In late September 1969, the song became The Monkees' final charting B-side, bubbling under the Hot 100 at #109.

Micky Dolenz: "That was one of my favorites. I was going through a period of social revelation. I have a lot of Indian heritage, so that had something to do with it. That was a period when everybody was writing protest songs. I remember sitting there writing it in my littl house up in Laurel Canyon on my mom's old piano. Making my little statement. I'v got to hand it to Mike. Mike was the one that came out and said, 'Micky, you shoul start writing and putting your stuff on these albums.' He was doing it also so tha would support him in his fight. He said, 'Put it on.' I said, 'Well, I don't write.' He said, 'Ju write anything. Do it, we'll help you.' He was very supportive."

Peter Tork: "'Mommy And Daddy' was a real interesting song. I'm not sure that I think goes in quite the right direction musically, but (there are) some really interesting b on it."

Historical note: The single release of "Mommy And Daddy" featured Dolenz's secon draft lyrics. His first set didn't get past Lester Sill, though the outtake version we eventually made part of the CD reissue of *The Monkees Present*.

Micky Dolenz: "I often wondered what happened to that version. Lester Sill said, 'Micky, you cannot do this.' I really wanted to put that out."

14. GOOD CLEAN FUN

After the positive response to "Listen To The Band," another Nesmith Nashville track was pulled as a follow-up single. "Good Clean Fun" is even more country-influenced and perhaps even less accessible. With no mention of the song's title anywhere in the song's lyrics, it was impossible to call in and request for radio, and even harder to ask for by name in a record store. Needless to say, it was not a big seller. Two weeks after its release, "Good Clean Fun" slid onto the charts for a mere five weeks, eventually reaching #82.

Michael Nesmith: "That was a direct insult to a songwriter publisher who had told me that in order to have successful tunes I had to write music that was good, clean fun and that had a recurring theme or hook line. Of course, I just rejected that out of hand. (I thought) *OK, I'll write a song called 'Good Clean Fun.' I just won't put it in there anywhere.* That's poetic license. It happens to be studied. It's not natural to me. I think, *Hmm, I wonder what obscure piece of business I can put on this sucker.* It has to do with being contrary and perverse. In some instances that's why I do that."

15. LOOKING FOR THE GOOD TIMES

The Monkees' eighth album, *The Monkees Present,* is similar to *Instant Replay* in that it features a hodgepodge of tracks from sessions between 1966 and 1969. The results are predictably mixed, though some good tracks were featured on the set. One of these is Boyce & Hart's "Looking For The Good Times," a song taped at the same session as "Teardrop City" in October 1966.

16. STEAM ENGINE

As the 1960s drew to a close, The Monkees decreased in number once again when Michael Nesmith left to start The First National Band. Meanwhile, CBS had begun running TV series in reruns for the Saturday-morning cartoon audience. Interestingly, these reruns featured the show's romps redubbed with newer material in an effort to update The Monkees' image and promote their newer releases. In addition to some older outtakes that were finally utilized on these shows, a brand-new song called "Steam Engine" (which was written and produced

by Chip Douglas) popped up in a few broadcasts. Unfortunately, the song's big production amounted to an even bigger studio bill, and when Screen Gems heard i was going to have to pay $5,000 for one finished song, they refused. Ultimately, they ended up splitting the costs with Douglas, but never got around to issuing the song on record.

Chip Douglas: "That was the famous session where I had to pay for half of it, 'cause i cost so much money. Which later worked out pretty well because it gave me a star on a publishing company. Lester Sill called me up and said they'd never had a cor tract signed on it. I said, 'Well, since you guys made me pay for half of it, we'll split the publishing.' It's a strange song; you know, it's sort of embarrassing looking back on i' I had this strange little fantasy of a guy chasing a train that his girlfriend is on. I don' know what got me thinking of it. It's just something that popped into my head. I like mechanical things. I never went riding on any trains or anything, but I grew up witl them. On the plantation where I grew up (in Hawaii), there were always these little steam trains that would carry the cane from the fields into the mill. I guess that migh have had something to do with it. Actually, it's incomplete. It has a third verse that never wrote until I was requested to get a lead sheet to Screen Gems."

17. I NEVER THOUGHT IT PECULIAR

Boyce & Hart's "I Never Thought It Peculiar" also turned up on a Saturday-mornin rerun soundtrack. However, unlike "Steam Engine," this song was released. It was last-minute addition to the group's 1970 long-player, *Changes*, though the song itse dated back to the prolific 1966 *More Of The Monkees* sessions.

Tommy Boyce: "That was kind of an English-oriented song. In the middle we decide to put a Jimi Hendrix guitar solo in there just for fun. We just sort of did what we felt i those days. We liked to experiment a lot. If we liked it, we figured maybe othe people might like it. I always thought that should have been a single."

18. MIDNIGHT TRAIN

Micky Dolenz's "Midnight Train" had been demoed all the way back in early 1967 c a session for *Headquarters*. Nevertheless, Dolenz didn't get around to making full-fledged version of the song until July 1969. "Midnight Train" was another Saturda morning favorite that slid onto *Changes* at the last minute.

Micky Dolenz: "I must have written that when I was like 16 years old or so. My sist Coco and I used to sing together, not so much professionaly, we just used to sin When The Monkees came around a few years later I recorded that, and she san on the record. There's not any inspiration so to speak, an event or anything, it's ju that I grew up on a diet of the Kingston Trio and people like that. I used to have litt folk-guitar groups and sing when I was younger, so that's where that came from."

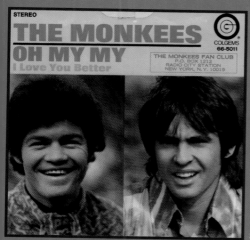

19. OH MY MY

As The Monkees crept into 1970, only Davy and Micky remained, and enthusiasm from Screen Gems to make more records was waning. They sent the duo to New York City in February 1970 to make a quickie album with Jeff Barry. At the time, Barry was making literally three or four records at once, and the individual creativity of Micky and Davy as performers was not a high priority. The results were respectable, if uninspired. The hardest-hitting track from the sessions, "Oh My My," was issued as a single but reached only #98, despite the fact that it was accompanied by an early music video.

Micky Dolenz: "That was my idea. That was my first music video that I produced and directed along with this cameraman. It was my idea to have horses and motorcycles and the similarities between. (A) 'ride that steel pony' kind of thing. I haven't seen that in years. That was when I was starting to get into production. Ricky Cooper shot some stuff and I was shooting stuff with my little 16-mm."

Davy Jones: "That was an effort to do something that was Monkees-esque. I think we had a $3,000-dollar budget. (We) rode our motorbikes around the desert and along the roads. We just tried to put together something general. We didn't go into the elaborate sort of video situation that they do now. It was all they wanted us to do. They were winding us down."

Andy Kim

Photo: MichaelOchsArchives.com

20. I LOVE YOU BETTER

Jeff Barry and Andy Kim both wrote "Oh My My" and its flip side, "I Love You Better." Davy contends these songs were merely backing tracks for another unfinished project that Jeff Barry had The Monkees randomly dub their voices onto.

Davy Jones: "That was Andy Kim and Jeff Barry doing an Andy Kim album. Andy Kim couldn't get it sold, so they took his voice off it, and they put us on it. That's how the came about. That was such a con. That was a way of keeping Micky Dolenz and I ou of the studio so they could sell Partridge Family albums. I have very bad memorie about that trip to New York."

21. DO YOU FEEL IT TOO?

Despite Davy's criticisms, he turns in a fine vocal performance on Jeff Barry and And Kim's "Do You Feel It Too?" This song, like several others from the *Changes* album, brief found its way onto the soundtrack of the Saturday-morning reruns. Nonetheless, th added promotion did little to boost the album chartwise. In fact, *Changes* was the fir Monkees album to entirely miss the *Billboard* Album chart, though it would finally cha when it was reissued on vinyl by Rhino Records in 1986.

22. DO IT IN THE NAME OF LOVE - Micky Dolenz & Davy Jones

The Monkees made one last trip into the recording studio during 1970. A session

September produced just two songs, the results of which were issued as a single on the Bell label under the name of Mickey Dolenz and Davy Jones. The A-side was Bobby Bloom and Neil Goldberg's "Do It In The Name Of Love."

23. THAT WAS THEN, THIS IS NOW
- Micky Dolenz & Peter Tork

Miraculously, The Monkees returned in 1986 with a sold-out tour, reruns of their series on MTV, and some new recordings. Technically these new tracks featured only Micky on lead vocals, with a small amount of partici-pation from Peter. Michael was not active in the 1986 reunion, and Davy refused to be involved in the recordings based on some ill feelings toward Arista Records. The record-ing sessions went ahead regardless and produced three new tunes for a best-of album called *Then & Now*. Vance Brescia's "That Was Then, This Is Now" (which gave the album its title) was pulled as a single and became The Monkees' first Top 20 hit since "D.W. Washburn" 18 years earlier.

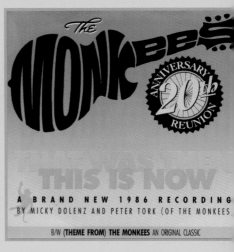

Micky Dolenz: "When they found out we were going on tour they came to us individually. They said, 'Do you want to record new songs? We're putting together a compilation album, and we want four new tunes on it.' I thought it was a marvelous opportunity. In fact, I think they approached me before I even started rehearsals. I thought it was a done deal. I said, 'I'll want more money.' They said, 'Fine, we'll rene-gotiate on the new tunes.' Then I heard as time went on that Davy wasn't making a deal. He wasn't returning phone calls. He was having a real big problem. Peter was also. He said, 'I don't like this song'—the same old stuff. I certainly wasn't going to put the kibosh on the deal because of Peter's problems or Davy's. That wouldn't have been right. Indeed Peter showed up at the session only out of my badgering. Davy never even showed up. Basically he couldn't make a deal for whatever reasons, and I did the songs."

24. HEART AND SOUL

Davy, Peter, and Micky all participated in the group's next official recording project: the 1987 album, *Pool It!* However, with extensive tour rehearsal obligations on deck, their participation was limited to a vocals-only role on most of the tracks. Perhaps the best recording from the project is "Heart And Soul," a song hand-picked by producer Roger Bechirian. As a single it became a minor chart hit in

September 1987, though it was hindered by a lack of MTV exposure as well as a competing chart song of the same title.

Peter Tork: "That was a very good album. Bechirian did a great job. Basically everything was solid and locked in the groove, and you really had the sense of being in the hands of a master. It may not have been genius, but it was very, very good."

25. MGBGT (Live)

Peter Tork scored the flip side of "Heart And Soul" with a song about his beloved car "MGBGT." The track came from a live performance by the band and was not included on *Pool It!*

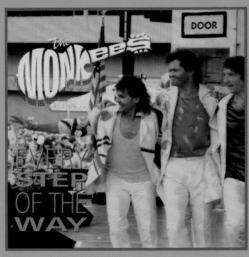

26. EVERY STEP OF THE WAY (Single Version)

The second single from *Pool It!* was Ian Hunter and Mark Clarke's "Every Step Of The Way." Hunter was a former member of Mott The Hoople and had recorded the song for his 1983 solo album, *All Of The Good Ones Are Taken*. Mark Clarke was the bassist with the band Colosseum and later toured with various ensembles including The Monkees. The single version was specially remixed for release but did not chart.

27. OH, WHAT A NIGHT

All four Monkees were present to record their final album as a group: *Justus*. This 1996 collection was entirely written, performed, and produced by Mike, Micky, Peter, and Davy à la *Headquarters*. Davy Jones brought several excellent songs to the project and his "Oh, What A Night" is a good example of the maturation of his songwriting talent. The track is highlighted by a great vocal harmony sound from the group. Unlike their previous reunion recordings (and some of their '60s efforts), The Monkees freely contributed vocals on one another's songs for *Justus*.

28. YOU AND I

Another of the album's highlights is Micky and Davy's "You And I." Originally, a dirgelike version of this song had appeared on 1976's *Dolenz, Jones, Boyce & Hart* album. The much-improved *Justus* remake is a refreshing lyrical reaffirmation of friendship for The Monkees as a group. Musically, the song is notable for some of Peter's best bass playing on record as well as for the welcome return of Nesmith's Gretsch 12-string guitar.

Micky Dolenz: "Davy and I wrote it on the freeway coming back from a show (with) Dolenz, Jones, Boyce & Hart at Knott's Berry Farm. It's one of the finest songs I've ever written, I think. I mean, it is really a together tune."

—Andrew Sandoval

Photo: Jay Silverman

1. **(THEME FROM) THE MONKEES**
(Tommy Boyce/Bobby Hart)
Produced by TOMMY BOYCE, BOBBY HART & JACK KELLER
Engineered by HANK CICALO
Recorded at RCA VICTOR STUDIO A, Hollywood, CA (7/19/66)
Featuring/MICKY DOLENZ: *lead vocals* • BOBBY HART & MICHEL RUBINI: *organ* • WAYNE ERWIN: *guitar, backing vocals* • GERRY McGEE & LOUIE SHELTON: *guitar* • LARRY TAYLOR: *bass* • BILLY LEWIS: *drums* • GENE ESTES: *tambourine* • TOMMY BOYCE, BOBBY HART & RON HICKLIN: *backing vocals*
From the album **The Monkees (A)** (10/66)

2. **I WANNA BE FREE (Fast Version)**
(Tommy Boyce/Bobby Hart)
Produced by TOMMY BOYCE & BOBBY HART
Engineered by HANK CICALO & HENRY LEWY
Recorded at RCA VICTOR STUDIO A, Hollywood, CA (7/19/66 & 7/24/66)
Featuring/MICKY DOLENZ & DAVY JONES: *lead vocals* • BOBBY HART & MICHEL RUBINI: *organ* • WAYNE ERWIN, GERRY McGEE & LOUIE SHELTON: *guitar* • LARRY TAYLOR: *bass* • BILLY LEWIS: *drums* • GENE ESTES: *tambourine*
Originally unissued • First collected on the album **Missing Links, Volume Two (U)** (1/23/90)

3. **LET'S DANCE ON**
(Tommy Boyce/Bobby Hart)
Produced by TOMMY BOYCE, BOBBY HART & JACK KELLER
Engineer(s) unknown
Recorded at RCA VICTOR STUDIO A, Hollywood, CA (7/5/66, 7/9/66 & 7/11/66)
Featuring/MICKY DOLENZ: *lead vocals* • BOBBY HART: *organ, backing vocals* • WAYNE ERWIN, GERRY McGEE & LOUIE SHELTON: *guitar* • BILLY LEWIS: *drums* • TOMMY BOYCE & RON HICKLIN: *backing vocals*
From the album **The Monkees (A)** (10/66)

Disc 1

1966

4. **LAST TRAIN TO CLARKSVILLE**
(Tommy Boyce/Bobby Hart)
Produced by TOMMY BOYCE & BOBBY HART
Engineered by DAVID HASSINGER
Recorded at RCA VICTOR STUDIO B, Hollywood, CA (7/25/66)
Featuring/MICKY DOLENZ: *lead vocals* • TOMMY BOYCE: *acoustic guitar* • WAYNE ERWIN, GERRY McGEE & LOUIE SHELTON: *guitar* • LARRY TAYLOR: *bass* • BILLY LEWIS: *drums* • GENE ESTES: *percussion* • Unknown *backing vocals*
Originally issued as Colgems single #1001 (8/16/66); *Pop #1* • Also included on the album **The Monkees (A)** (10/66)

5. **TAKE A GIANT STEP**
(Carole King/Gerry Goffin)
Produced by TOMMY BOYCE & BOBBY HART
Engineered by HANK CICALO
Recorded at RCA VICTOR STUDIO A, Hollywood, CA (7/9/66)
Featuring/MICKY DOLENZ: *vocals* • JACK KELLER: *piano* • MICHEL RUBINI: *harpsichord* • WAYNE ERWIN, GERRY McGEE & LOUIE SHELTON: *electric guitar* • TOMMY BOYCE: *acoustic guitar* • LARRY TAYLOR: *bass* • BILLY LEWIS: *drums* • BOBBY HART: *glockenspiel* • GENE ESTES: *percussion* • BOB COOPER: *oboe*
Originally issued as Colgems single #1001 (8/16/66) • Also included on the album **The Monkees (A)** (10/66)

6. **ALL THE KING'S HORSES**
(Michael Nesmith)
Produced by MICHAEL NESMITH
Engineered by DAVID HASSINGER (& others)
Recorded at RCA VICTOR STUDIO A, Hollywood, CA (6/25/66, 7/11/66 & 7/16/66)
Featuring/MICKY DOLENZ & MICHAEL NESMITH: *lead vocals* • JAMES BURTON, GLEN CAMPBELL & AL CASEY: *guitar* • LARRY KNECHTEL & BOB WEST: *bass* • HAL BLAINE & JIM GORDON: *drums* • GARY COLEMAN: *percussion* • DONALD PEAKE: *arrangement* • DAVY JONES & PETER TORK: *backing vocals*

Originally unissued • First collected on the album **Missing Links, Volume Two (U)** (1/23/90)

7. **SATURDAY'S CHILD**
(David Gates)
Produced by TOMMY BOYCE, BOBBY HART & JACK KELLER
Engineered by HANK CICALO
Recorded at RCA VICTOR STUDIO A, Hollywood, C (7/9/66)
Featuring/MICKY DOLENZ: *lead vocals* • WAYNE ERWIN: *guitar, backing vocals* • GERRY McGEE & LOUIE SHELTON: *guitar* • LARRY TAYLOR: *bass* • BILLY LEWIS: *drums* • GENE ESTES: *tambourine* • TOMMY BOYCE, BOBBY HART & RON HICKLIN: *backing vocals*
From the album **The Monkees (A)** (10/66)

8. **PAPA GENE'S BLUES**
(Michael Nesmith)
Produced by MICHAEL NESMITH
Engineered by DAVID HASSINGER (& others)
Recorded at WESTERN RECORDERS STUDIO, Hollywood, CA (7/7/66) • RCA VICTOR STUDIO, Hollywood, CA (7/11/66, 7/16/66 & 7/30/66)
Featuring/MICHAEL NESMITH: *lead vocals* • MICKY DOLENZ: *harmony vocals* • JAMES BURTON, GLEN CAMPBELL, AL CASEY, JIMMY HELMS, BILL PITMAN & PETER TORK: *guitar* • HAL BLAINE & JIM GORDON: *drums* • GARY COLEMAN & FRANK DeVITO: *percussion* • DONALD PEAKE: *arrangement* • Unknown *bass*
From the album **The Monkees (A)** (10/66)

9. **I WANNA BE FREE (Album Version)**
(Tommy Boyce/Bobby Hart)
Produced by TOMMY BOYCE & BOBBY HART
Engineered by HANK CICALO & HENRY LEWY
Recorded at RCA VICTOR STUDIO A, Hollywood, C (7/19/66 & 7/24/66)
Featuring/DAVY JONES: *lead vocals* • MICHEL RUBINI: *harpsichord* • GERRY McGEE & LOUIE SHELTON: *acoustic guitar* • BONNIE DOUGLAS & PA SHURE: *violin* • MYRA KESTENBAUM: *viola* • FREDERICK SEYKORA: *cello*
From the album **The Monkees (A)** (10/66)

10. **SWEET YOUNG THING**
(Michael Nesmith/Carole King/Gerry Goffin)
Produced by MICHAEL NESMITH
Engineered by HANK CICALO & HENRY LEWY
Recorded at RCA VICTOR STUDIO A, Hollywood, C (7/18/66) • RCA VICTOR STUDIO B, Hollywood, C (7/27/66)
Featuring/MICHAEL NESMITH: *lead vocals* • JAMES BURTON, GLEN CAMPBELL, AL CASEY & MIKE DEASY: *guitar* • JIMMY BRYANT: *fiddle* • LARRY KNECHTEL & BOB WEST: *bass* • HAL BLAINE & JIM GORDON: *drums* • GARY COLEMAN & FRANK DeVITO: *percussion* • MICKY DOLENZ: *backing vocals* • DONALD PEAKE: *arrangement* • Unknown *Danelectro bass*
From the album **The Monkees (A)** (10/66)

11. **GONNA BUY ME A DOG**
(Tommy Boyce/Bobby Hart)
Produced by TOMMY BOYCE, BOBBY HART & JACK KELLER
Engineered by DAVID HASSINGER & RICHIE SCHMITT
Recorded at RCA VICTOR STUDIO A, Hollywood, C (7/23/66 & 7/24/66)
Featuring/MICKY DOLENZ & DAVY JONES: *lead vocals* • BOBBY HART: *organ* • WAYNE ERWIN, GERRY McGEE & LOUIE SHELTON: *guitar* • LARRY TAYLOR: *bass* • BILLY LEWIS: *drums*
From the album **The Monkees (A)** (10/66)

12. **I DON'T THINK YOU KNOW ME (First Recorded Version)**
(Gerry Goffin/Carole King)
Produced by MICHAEL NESMITH
Engineered by DAVID HASSINGER (& others)
Recorded at RCA VICTOR STUDIO A, Hollywood, (6/25/66 & 7/16/66) • RCA VICTOR STUDIO Hollywood, CA (8/30/66)
Featuring/MICHAEL NESMITH: *lead vocals* • JAMES BURTON, GLEN CAMPBELL & AL CASEY: *guitar* • LARRY KNECHTEL & BOB WEST: *bass* • HAL BLAINE & JIM GORDON: *drums* • GARY COLEMAN: *percussion* • DONALD PEAKE: *arrangement* • Unknown *backing vocals*
Originally unissued • First collected on the album **Missing Links (R)** (7/6/87)

13. **I'M A BELIEVER**
(Neil Diamond)
Produced by JEFF BARRY
Engineer(s) unknown
Recorded at RCA VICTOR STUDIO B, New York, NY
(10/15/66) • RCA VICTOR STUDIO B, Hollywood,
CA (10/23/66)
Featuring/MICKY DOLENZ: lead vocals • Other
personnel unknown
Originally issued as Colgems single #1002 (11/12/66);
Pop #1 • Also included on the album *More Of
The Monkees* **(B)** (1/10/67)

14. **(I'M NOT YOUR) STEPPIN' STONE**
(Tommy Boyce/Bobby Hart)
Produced by TOMMY BOYCE & BOBBY HART
Engineered by HENRY LEWY
Recorded at WESTERN RECORDERS STUDIO 1, Hollywood,
CA (7/26/66)
Featuring/MICKY DOLENZ: lead vocals • BOBBY HART:
organ • WAYNE ERWIN: guitar, backing vocals •
GERRY McGEE & LOUIE SHELTON: guitar • LARRY
TAYLOR: bass • BILLY LEWIS: drums • TOMMY
BOYCE & BOBBY HART: backing vocals • Unknown
percussion
Originally issued as Colgems single #1002 (11/12/66);
Pop #20 • Also included on the album *More Of
The Monkees* **(B)** (1/10/67)

15. **SHE**
(Tommy Boyce/Bobby Hart)
Produced by TOMMY BOYCE & BOBBY HART
Engineer(s) unknown
Recorded at RCA VICTOR STUDIO A, Hollywood, CA
(8/15/66) • RCA VICTOR STUDIO B, Hollywood, CA
(8/27/66)
Featuring/MICKY DOLENZ: lead vocals • BOBBY HART:
organ • WAYNE ERWIN, GERRY McGEE & LOUIE
SHELTON: guitar • LARRY TAYLOR: bass • BILLY
LEWIS: drums • NORM JEFFRIES: percussion •
TOMMY BOYCE, WAYNE ERWIN, BOBBY HART &
RON HICKLIN: backing vocals
From the album *More Of The Monkees* **(B)** (1/10/67)

16. **MARY, MARY**
(Michael Nesmith)
Produced by MICHAEL NESMITH
Engineered by ANDY R., HENRY LEWY, HANK CICALO &
RICHIE SCHMITT
Recorded at WESTERN RECORDERS STUDIO 2, Hollywood,
CA (7/25/66) • RCA VICTOR STUDIO B, Hollywood,
CA (7/27/66 & 10/18/66)
Featuring/MICKY DOLENZ: lead vocals • MICHAEL
COHEN & LARRY KNECHTEL: keyboards • JAMES
BURTON, GLEN CAMPBELL, AL CASEY, MIKE DEASY &
PETER TORK: guitar • BOB WEST: bass • HAL BLAINE:
drums • GARY COLEMAN & JIM GORDON:
percussion • DONALD PEAKE: arrangement
From the album *More Of The Monkees* **(B)** (1/10/67)

17. **YOUR AUNTIE GRIZELDA**
(Jack Keller/Diane Hilderbrand)
Produced by JEFF BARRY & JACK KELLER
Engineered by RICHARD PODOLOR (& others)
Recorded at AMERICAN RECORDING CO., Studio City,
CA (10/14/66) • RCA VICTOR STUDIO B, Hollywood,
CA (10/23/66)
Featuring/PETER TORK: lead vocals • Other personnel
unknown
From the album *More Of The Monkees* **(B)** (1/10/67)

18. **OF YOU (Previously Unissued Mix)**
(Bill Chadwick/John Chadwick)
Produced by MICHAEL NESMITH
Engineered by ANDY R. & HENRY LEWY
Recorded at WESTERN RECORDERS STUDIO 2, Hollywood,
CA (7/25/66) • RCA VICTOR STUDIO B, Hollywood,
CA (7/27/66)
Featuring/MICHAEL NESMITH: lead vocals • MICKY
DOLENZ: harmony vocals • MICHAEL COHEN &
LARRY KNECHTEL: keyboards • JAMES BURTON,
GLEN CAMPBELL, AL CASEY, MIKE DEASY & PETER
TORK: guitar • BOB WEST: bass • HAL BLAINE:
drums • GARY COLEMAN & JIM GORDON:
percussion • DONALD PEAKE: arrangement
Previously unissued • An alternate mix was first
collected on the album *Missing Links*

19. **LOOK OUT (HERE COMES
TOMORROW)
(Previously Unissued Extended Version)**
(Neil Diamond)
Produced by JEFF BARRY
Engineered by HANK CICALO (& others)
Recorded at RCA VICTOR STUDIO B, New York, NY
(10/15/66 & 10/23/66) • RCA VICTOR STUDIO A,
Hollywood, CA (10/26/66)
Featuring/DAVY JONES: lead vocals • Other personnel
unknown
Previously unissued • An edited version was included
on the album *More Of The Monkees*

20. **THE KIND OF GIRL I COULD LOVE**
(Michael Nesmith/Roger Atkins)
Produced by MICHAEL NESMITH
Engineered by DAVID HASSINGER (& others)
Recorded at RCA VICTOR STUDIO A, Hollywood, CA
(6/25/66, 7/11/66, 7/16/66 & 7/30/66)
Featuring/MICHAEL NESMITH: lead vocals • JAMES
BURTON, GLEN CAMPBELL & AL CASEY: guitar •
LARRY KNECHTEL & BOB WEST: bass • HAL BLAINE
& JIM GORDON: drums • GARY COLEMAN:
percussion • MICKY DOLENZ, DAVY JONES &
PETER TORK: backing vocals • DONALD PEAKE:
arrangement
From the album *More Of The Monkees* **(B)** (1/10/67)

21. **SOMETIME IN THE MORNING**
(Gerry Goffin/Carole King)
Produced by GERRY GOFFIN, CAROLE KING & JEFF BARRY
Engineered by HANK CICALO (& others)
Recorded at RCA VICTOR STUDIO A, New York, NY
(10/13/66 & 10/25/66) • RCA VICTOR STUDIOS,
Hollywood, CA (10/27/66)
Featuring/MICKY DOLENZ: lead vocals • Other
personnel unknown
From the album *More Of The Monkees* **(B)** (1/10/67)

22. **WHEN LOVE COMES KNOCKIN'
(AT YOUR DOOR)**
(Neil Sedaka/Carole Bayer)
Produced by NEIL SEDAKA & CAROLE BAYER
Engineered by ERNIE OELRICH
Recorded at RCA VICTOR STUDIO A, New York, NY
(11/23/66)
Featuring/DAVY JONES: lead vocals • NEIL SEDAKA:
piano • ALEXANDER GAFA, BILL SUYKER & DON
THOMAS: guitar • RUSS SAVAKUS: bass • HERB
LOVELLE: drums • Unknown percussion
From the album *More Of The Monkees* **(B)** (1/10/67)

23. **DO NOT ASK FOR LOVE
(First Recorded Version)**
(Michael Martin Murphey)
Produced by MICHAEL NESMITH
Engineered by ANDY R., HENRY LEWY, HANK CICALO &
RICHIE SCHMITT
Recorded at WESTERN RECORDERS STUDIO 2,
Hollywood, CA (7/25/66) • RCA VICTOR STUDIO
B, Hollywood, CA (7/27/66 & 10/18/66)
Featuring/MICKY DOLENZ: lead & backing vocals •
MICHAEL COHEN & LARRY KNECHTEL: keyboards •
JAMES BURTON, GLEN CAMPBELL, AL CASEY,
MIKE DEASY & PETER TORK: guitar • BOB WEST:
bass • HAL BLAINE & JIM GORDON: drums •
GARY COLEMAN: percussion • DONALD PEAKE:
arrangement
Originally unissued • First collected on the album
Missing Links, Volume Two **(U)** (1/23/90)

24. **VALLERI (First Recorded Version)**
(Tommy Boyce/Bobby Hart)
Produced by TOMMY BOYCE & BOBBY HART
Engineered by HANK CICALO & HENRY LEWY
Recorded at RCA VICTOR STUDIO A, Hollywood, CA
(8/6/66) • RCA VICTOR STUDIO B, Hollywood, CA
(8/27/66)
Featuring/DAVY JONES: lead vocals • BOBBY HART:
keyboards, backing vocals • WAYNE ERWIN:
guitar, backing vocals • JERRY McGEE & LOUIE
SHELTON: guitar • LARRY TAYLOR: bass • BILLY
LEWIS: drums • GENE ESTES: percussion • TOMMY
BOYCE & RON HICKLIN: backing vocals
Originally unissued • First collected on the album
Missing Links, Volume Two **(U)** (1/23/90)

25. **I'LL BE BACK UPON MY FEET
(First Recorded Version)**
(Sandy Linzer/Denny Randall)
Produced by JEFF BARRY
Engineered by HANK CICALO
Recorded at RCA VICTOR STUDIO A, Hollywood, CA
(10/28/66)
Featuring/MICKY DOLENZ: lead & backing vocals •
DON RANDI & MICHEL RUBINI: keyboards • AL
CASEY: guitar • CAROL KAYE & RAY POHLMAN:
bass • HAL BLAINE: drums • FRANK CAPP &
JULIUS WECHTER: percussion
Originally unissued • First collected on the album
Missing Links, Volume Two **(U)** (1/23/90)

1. **A LITTLE BIT ME, A LITTLE BIT YOU**
(Neil Diamond)
Produced by JEFF BARRY
Engineered by RAY HALL
Recorded at RCA VICTOR STUDIO B, New York, NY (1/21/67,
2/4/67 & 2/6/67)
Featuring/DAVY JONES: *lead vocals* • STAN FREE: *clavinet* •
ARTIE BUTLER: *organ* • AL GORGONI, HUGH
McCRACKEN & DON THOMAS: *guitar* • LOUIS MAURO
& JAMES TYRELL: *bass* • HERB LOVELLE: *drums* • TOM
CERONE: *tambourine* • JEFF BARRY: *arrangement* •
Unknown *hand claps & backing vocals*
Originally issued as Colgems single #1004 (3/8/67);
Pop #2 • First collected on the album **The Monkees
Greatest Hits (H)** (6/69)

2. **SHE HANGS OUT**
(Single Version)
(Jeff Barry)
Produced by JEFF BARRY
Engineered by RAY HALL
Music Supervision: DON KIRSHNER
Recorded at RCA VICTOR STUDIO B, New York, NY (1/21/67,
2/4/67, 2/5/67 & 2/6/67)
Featuring/DAVY JONES: *lead vocals* • ARTIE BUTLER:
organ • STAN FREE: *clavinet* • AL GORGONI, HUGH
McCRACKEN & DON THOMAS: *guitar* • LOUIS MAURO
& JAMES TYRELL: *bass* • HERB LOVELLE: *drums* • TOM
CERONE: *tambourine* • JEFF BARRY: *arrangement* •
Unknown *backing vocals*
Originally issued as Colgems (Canada) single #1003
(2/67) (withdrawn) • First collected on the albums
**Monkeemania: 40 Timeless Hits From The
Monkees (N)** (10/79) & **Monkee Business (O)**
(11/82)

3. **THE GIRL I KNEW SOMEWHERE**
(Michael Nesmith)
Produced by DOUGLAS FARTHING HATLELID
Engineered by HANK CICALO
Recorded at RCA VICTOR STUDIO A, Hollywood, CA
(2/23/67)
Featuring/MICKY DOLENZ: *lead &
backing vocals, drums* • PETER TORK:
harpsichord, backing vocals •
MICHAEL NESMITH: *electric guitar,
acoustic 12-string guitar, backing
vocals* • JOHN LONDON: *bass,
tambourine*
Originally issued as Colgems single
#1004 (3/8/67); *Pop #39* • First col-
lected on the album **The Monkees
(M)** (7/76)

4. **ALL OF YOUR TOYS**
(Bill Martin)
Produced by DOUGLAS FARTHING HATLELID
Engineered by DICK BOGERT, RICHIE SCHMITT & HANK
CICALO
Recorded at RCA VICTOR STUDIO A, Hollywood, CA
(1/16/67 & 1/19/67) • RCA VICTOR STUDIO B,
Hollywood, CA (1/30/67 & 1/31/67)
Featuring/MICKY DOLENZ: *lead vocals, drums* • PETER
TORK: *harpsichord, backing vocals* • MICHAEL
NESMITH: *electric 12-string guitar, backing vocals* •
JOHN LONDON: *bass* • DAVY JONES: *tambourine,
backing vocals*
Originally unissued • First collected on the album **Missing
Links (R)** (7/6/87)

5. **LOVE TO LOVE**
(Neil Diamond)
Produced by JEFF BARRY
Engineered by RAY HALL (& others)
Recorded at RCA VICTOR STUDIO B, New York, NY (1/21/67,
2/4/67 & 2/5/67) • RCA VICTOR STUDIOS, Hollywood,
CA (8/5/69)
Featuring/DAVY JONES: *lead vocals* • ARTIE BUTLER:
organ • STAN FREE: *clavinet* • AL GORGONI, HUGH
McCRACKEN & DON THOMAS: *guitar* • LOUIS MAURO
& JAMES TYRELL: *bass* • HERB LOVELLE: *drums* • TOM
CERONE: *tambourine*
Originally unissued • First collected on the albums
**Monkeemania: 40 Timeless Hits From The
Monkees (N)** (10/79) & **Monkee Business (O)**
(11/82)

6. **YOU TOLD ME**
(Michael Nesmith)
Produced by DOUGLAS FARTHING HATLELID
Engineered by HANK CICALO
Recorded at RCA VICTOR STUDIO B, Hollywood, CA
(3/3/67) • RCA VICTOR STUDIO C, Hollywood, CA
(3/9/67)
Featuring/MICHAEL NESMITH: *lead vocals, 12-string guitar* •
PETER TORK: *banjo, backing vocals* • MICKY DOLENZ:

zither, drums, backing vocals • CHIP DOUGLAS
bass • DAVY JONES: *tambourine, backing vocals*
From the album **Headquarters (C)** (5/22/67)

7. **I'LL SPEND MY LIFE WITH YOU**
(Tommy Boyce/Bobby Hart)
Produced by DOUGLAS FARTHING HATLELID
Engineered by HANK CICALO
Recorded at RCA VICTOR STUDIO C, Hollywood, C
(3/4/67, 3/9/67, 3/11/67 & 3/18/67)
Featuring/MICKY DOLENZ: *lead vocals, electric guitar*
PETER TORK: *harmony vocals, organ, celest
acoustic 12-string guitar* • MICHAEL NESMITH: *ped
steel guitar* • CHIP DOUGLAS: *bass* • DAVY JONE
tambourine*
From the album **Headquarters (C)** (5/22/67)

8. **FORGET THAT GIRL**
(Douglas Farthing Hatlelid)
Produced by DOUGLAS FARTHING HATLELID
Engineered by HANK CICALO
Recorded at RCA VICTOR STUDIO B, Hollywood, C
(3/2/67) • RCA VICTOR STUDIO C, Hollywood, C
(3/7/67, 3/8/67 & 3/10/67)
Featuring/DAVY JONES: *lead & backing voca
maracas* • PETER TORK: *electric piano, backin
vocals* • MICHAEL NESMITH: *electric 12-string guita
CHIP DOUGLAS: *bass, backing vocals* • MIC
DOLENZ: *drums, backing vocals* • Unknow
acoustic guitar*
From the album **Headquarters (C)** (5/22/67)

9. **YOU JUST MAY BE THE ONE**
(Michael Nesmith)
Produced by DOUGLAS FARTHING HATLELID
Engineered by HANK CICALO
Recorded at RCA VICTOR STUDIO C, Hollywood, C
(3/16/67)
Featuring/MICHAEL NESMITH: *lead vocals, elect
12-string guitar* • PETER TORK: *double-tracked bas
MICKY DOLENZ: *drums, backing vocals* • DA
JONES: *tambourine, backing vocals* • CH
DOUGLAS: *backing vocals* • Unknown *acous
guitar*
From the album **Headquarters (C)** (5/22/67)

10. **SHADES OF GRAY**
(Barry Mann/Cynthia Weil)
Produced by DOUGLAS FARTHING HATLELID
Engineered by HANK CICALO
Recorded at RCA VICTOR STUDIO C, Hollywood,
(3/16/67, 3/22/67 & 3/23/67)
Featuring/PETER TORK: *lead vocals, piano* • DAVY JON
lead vocals, maracas • MICKY DOLENZ: *harmo
vocals, drums* • MICHAEL NESMITH: *pedal st
guitar* • JERRY YESTER: *bass* • VINCENT DeRO
French horn • FREDERICK SEYKORA: *cello*
From the album **Headquarters (C)** (5/22/67)

11. **FOR PETE'S SAKE**
(Peter Tork/Joseph Richards)
Produced by DOUGLAS FARTHING HATLELID
Engineered by HANK CICALO
Recorded at RCA VICTOR STUDIO C, Hollywood,
(3/23/67)
Featuring/MICKY DOLENZ: *lead vocals, drums* • MICH
NESMITH: *organ, electric 12-string guita
PETER TORK: *electric guitar, backing vocal
CHIP DOUGLAS: *bass* • DAVY JONES: *tambouri
backing vocals* • Unknown *additional elec
guitar*
From the album **Headquarters (C)** (5/22/67)

12. **SUNNY GIRLFRIEND**
(Michael Nesmith)
Produced by DOUGLAS FARTHING HATLELID
Engineered by HANK CICALO
Recorded at RCA VICTOR STUDIO A, Hollywood,
(2/23/67) • RCA VICTOR STUDIO C, Hollywood,
(4/18/67)
Featuring/MICHAEL NESMITH: *lead vocals, elec
12-string guitar, acoustic guitar* • MICKY DOL
harmony vocals, drums • PETER TORK: *ele
guitar* • JOHN LONDON: *bass* • DAVY JO
maracas, backing vocals
From the album **Headquarters (C)** (5/22/67)

13. **NO TIME**
(Hank Cicalo)
Produced by DOUGLAS FARTHING HATLELID
Engineered by HANK CICALO
Recorded at RCA VICTOR STUDIO C, Hollywood,
(3/28/67)
Featuring/MICKY DOLENZ: *lead vocals, drums* • P
TORK: *piano* • MICHAEL NESMITH: *electric gui
CHIP DOUGLAS: *bass* • DAVY JONES: *tambou
backing vocals* • Unknown *additional ele*

Disc 2

1967

33

guitar & backing vocals
From the album *Headquarters* **(C)** (5/22/67)

RANDY SCOUSE GIT
(Micky Dolenz)
Produced by DOUGLAS FARTHING HATLELID
Engineered by HANK CICALO
Recorded at RCA VICTOR STUDIO B, Hollywood, CA
(3/2/67) • RCA VICTOR STUDIO C, Hollywood, CA
(3/4/67 & 3/8/67)
Featuring/MICKY DOLENZ: *lead vocals, drums, tympani* •
PETER TORK: *piano, organ* • MICHAEL NESMITH:
electric 12-string guitar, backing vocals • CHIP
DOUGLAS: *bass* • DAVY JONES: *backing vocals*
From the album *Headquarters* **(C)** (5/22/67)

PLEASANT VALLEY SUNDAY
(Single Version)
(Gerry Goffin/Carole King)
Produced by CHIP DOUGLAS
Engineered by HANK CICALO
Recorded at RCA VICTOR STUDIO A, Hollywood, CA
(6/10/67, 6/11/67 & 6/13/67)
Featuring/MICKY DOLENZ: *lead vocals* • PETER TORK:
piano • MICHAEL NESMITH: *electric guitar, backing
vocals* • BILL CHADWICK: *acoustic guitar* • CHIP
DOUGLAS: *bass* • EDDIE HOH: *drums* • DAVY JONES:
backing vocals
Originally issued as Colgems single #1007 (7/10/67); *Pop
#3* • First collected on the album *Monkee Business*
(O) (11/82) • An alternate mix was included on the
album *Pisces, Aquarius, Capricorn & Jones Ltd.*

WORDS
(Tommy Boyce/Bobby Hart)
Produced by CHIP DOUGLAS
Engineered by HANK CICALO
Recorded at RCA VICTOR STUDIO A, Hollywood, CA
(6/14/67) • RCA VICTOR STUDIO C, Hollywood, CA
(6/15/67)
Featuring/MICKY DOLENZ: *lead & backing vocals* • PETER
TORK: *lead vocals, organ* • MICHAEL NESMITH:
tremolo electric guitar, backing vocals • CHIP
DOUGLAS: *bass* • EDDIE HOH: *drums* • DAVY JONES:
chimes, tree, backing vocals
Originally issued as Colgems single #1007 (7/10/67); *Pop
#11* • Also included on the album *Pisces,
Aquarius, Capricorn & Jones Ltd.* **(D)** (11/14/67)

DAYDREAM BELIEVER
(John Stewart)
Produced by CHIP DOUGLAS
Engineered by HANK CICALO
Recorded at RCA VICTOR STUDIO A, Hollywood, CA
(6/14/67 & 8/9/67)
Featuring/DAVY JONES: *lead vocals* • PETER TORK: *piano* •
MICHAEL NESMITH: *guitar* • CHIP DOUGLAS: *bass* •
EDDIE HOH: *drums* • BILL MARTIN: *percussion* •
BOBBY HELFER: *piccolo trumpet* • PETE CANDOLI, AL
PORCINO & MANUEL STEVENS: *trumpet* • RICHARD
NOEL: *trombone* • RICHARD LEITH & PHIL TEELE: *bass
trombone* • NATHAN KAPROFF, GEORGE KAST, ALEX
MURRAY & ERNO NEUFELD: *violin* • MICKY DOLENZ:
backing vocals • SHORTY ROGERS: *arrangement*
Originally issued as Colgems single #1012 (10/25/67);
Pop #1 • Also included on the album *The Birds,
The Bees & The Monkees* **(E)** (4/22/68)

GOIN' DOWN
*(Diane Hilderbrand/Peter Tork/Michael Nesmith/Micky
Dolenz/Davy Jones)*
Produced by CHIP DOUGLAS
Engineered by HANK CICALO
Recorded at RCA VICTOR STUDIO A, Hollywood, CA
(6/21/67 & 7/5/67) • RCA VICTOR STUDIOS,
Hollywood, CA (9/15/67)
Featuring/MICKY DOLENZ: *lead vocals* • MICHAEL
NESMITH & PETER TORK: *electric guitar* • CHIP
DOUGLAS: *bass* • EDDIE HOH: *drums* • BUD
BRISBOIS, VIRGIL EVANS, UAN RASEY & THOMAS
SCOTT: *trumpet* • BOBBY HELFER: *trumpet, bass clar-
inet* • LOU BLACKBURN & DICK NASH: *trombone* •
RICHARD LEITH & PHIL TEELE: *bass trombone* •
BUDDY COLLETTE, BILL HOOD & PLAS JOHNSON:
sax • JOHN LOWE: *bass sax* • SHORTY ROGERS:
arrangement • BILL MARTIN: *unknown*
Originally issued as Colgems single #1012 (10/25/67);
Pop #104 • First collected on the albums
*Monkeemania: 40 Timeless Hits From The
Monkees* **(N)** (10/79) & *Monkee Business* **(O)**
(11/82)

SALESMAN
(Craig Vincent Smith)
Produced by CHIP DOUGLAS

Engineered by HANK CICALO
Recorded at RCA VICTOR STUDIO A, Hollywood, CA
(6/14/67)
Featuring/MICHAEL NESMITH: *lead vocals, guitar* • CHIP
DOUGLAS: *nylon-string guitar, bass* • EDDIE HOH:
drums • MICKY DOLENZ & DAVY JONES: *percussion,
backing vocals*
From the album *Pisces, Aquarius, Capricorn & Jones
Ltd.* **(D)** (11/14/67)

20. ## THE DOOR INTO SUMMER
(Chip Douglas/Bill Martin)
Produced by CHIP DOUGLAS
Engineered by HANK CICALO
Recorded at RCA VICTOR STUDIOS A & C, Hollywood, CA
(5/29/67) • RCA VICTOR STUDIO B, Hollywood, CA
(8/23/67 & 8/24/67) • RCA VICTOR STUDIOS,
Hollywood, CA (9/7/67)
Featuring/MICHAEL NESMITH: *lead vocals* • MICKY
DOLENZ: *harmony vocals* • PETER TORK: *keyboards* •
CHIP DOUGLAS: *classical guitar* • LARRY TAYLOR:
bass • EDDIE HOH: *drums* • DAVY JONES: *backing
vocals* • DOUG DILLARD, BILL MARTIN & HARRY
NILSSON: *unknown*
From the album *Pisces, Aquarius, Capricorn & Jones
Ltd.* **(D)** (11/14/67)

21. ## LOVE IS ONLY SLEEPING
(Barry Mann/Cynthia Weil)
Produced by CHIP DOUGLAS
Engineered by HANK CICALO
Recorded at RCA VICTOR STUDIO C, Hollywood, CA
(6/19/67) • RCA VICTOR STUDIO A, Hollywood, CA
(7/10/67) • RCA VICTOR STUDIOS, Hollywood, CA
(9/7/67)
Featuring/MICHAEL NESMITH: *lead vocals, guitar* • PETER
TORK: *organ* • CHIP DOUGLAS: *guitar, bass* • EDDIE
HOH: *drums* • MICKY DOLENZ & DAVY JONES:
backing vocals • BILL MARTIN & HARRY NILSSON:
unknown
From the album *Pisces, Aquarius, Capricorn & Jones
Ltd.* **(D)** (11/14/67)

22. ## CUDDLY TOY
(Harry Nilsson)
Produced by CHIP DOUGLAS
Engineered by HANK CICALO
Recorded at RCA VICTOR STUDIOS, Hollywood, CA (4/67)
Featuring/DAVY JONES: *lead vocals, tambourine* • MICKY
DOLENZ: *harmony vocals, drums* • PETER TORK:
keyboards • MICHAEL NESMITH: *acoustic guitar* •
CHIP DOUGLAS: *bass* • EDGAR LUSTGARTEN: *cello* •
TED NASH, THOMAS SCOTT & BUD SHANK: *unknown*
From the album *Pisces, Aquarius, Capricorn & Jones
Ltd.* **(D)** (11/14/67)

23. ## WHAT AM I DOING HANGIN' 'ROUND?
(Michael Martin Murphey/Owen Castleman)
Produced by CHIP DOUGLAS
Engineered by HANK CICALO
Recorded at RCA VICTOR STUDIO A, Hollywood, CA
(6/20/67)
Featuring/MICHAEL NESMITH: *lead vocals, guitar* • PETER
TORK: *guitar* • DOUG DILLARD: *electric banjo* • CHIP
DOUGLAS: *bass* • EDDIE HOH: *drums* • MICKY
DOLENZ & DAVY JONES: *backing vocals*
From the album *Pisces, Aquarius, Capricorn & Jones
Ltd.* **(D)** (11/14/67)

24. ## DAILY NIGHTLY
(Michael Nesmith)
Produced by CHIP DOUGLAS
Engineered by HANK CICALO
Recorded at RCA VICTOR STUDIO C, Hollywood, CA
(6/19/67)
Featuring/MICKY DOLENZ: *lead vocals, Moog synthesizer* •
PETER TORK: *organ* • MICHAEL NESMITH: *guitar* • CHIP
DOUGLAS: *bass* • EDDIE HOH: *drums*
From the album *Pisces, Aquarius, Capricorn & Jones
Ltd.* **(D)** (11/14/67)

25. ## STAR COLLECTOR
(Gerry Goffin/Carole King)
Produced by CHIP DOUGLAS
Engineered by HANK CICALO
Recorded at RCA VICTOR STUDIO A, Hollywood, CA
(6/22/67 & 7/6/67) • AMERICAN RECORDING CO.,
Studio City, CA (10/4/67)
Featuring/DAVY JONES: *lead vocals* • PETER TORK: *key-
boards* • PAUL BEAVER: *Moog synthesizer* • MICHAEL
NESMITH: *guitar* • CHIP DOUGLAS: *bass* • EDDIE HOH:
drums • MICKY DOLENZ: *backing vocals* • BILL
MARTIN: *unknown*
From the album *Pisces, Aquarius, Capricorn & Jones
Ltd.* **(D)** (11/14/67)

1. **VALLERI**
(Tommy Boyce/Bobby Hart)
Produced by THE MONKEES
Engineered by HENRY LEWY
Recorded at UNITED RECORDERS STUDIO B, Hollywood,
CA (12/26/67) • UNITED RECORDERS, Hollywood,
CA (12/28/67) • Unknown studio, Hollywood,
CA (1/3/68)
Featuring/DAVY JONES: *lead vocals* • GERRY McGEE
& LOUIE SHELTON: *guitar* • JOE OSBORNE:
bass • BILLY LEWIS: *drums* • ROY CATON &
OLLIE MITCHELL: *trumpet* • LEW McCREARY:
trombone • JIM HORN & JAY MIGLIORI: *sax* •
DON McGINNIS: *arrangement* • Unknown
tambourine & backing vocals
Originally issued as Colgems single #1019 (3/2/68);
Pop #3 • Also included on the album *The Birds,
The Bees & The Monkees* **(E)** (4/22/68)

2. **TAPIOCA TUNDRA**
(Michael Nesmith)
Produced by THE MONKEES
Engineered by HANK CICALO
Recorded at RCA VICTOR STUDIOS, Hollywood, CA
(11/11/67)
Featuring/MICHAEL NESMITH: *lead vocals* • Other
personnel unknown
Originally issued as Colgems single #1019 (3/2/68);
Pop #34 • Also included on the album *The
Birds, The Bees & The Monkees* **(E)** (4/22/68)

3. **DREAM WORLD**
(Davy Jones/Steve Pitts)
Produced by THE MONKEES
Engineered by HANK CICALO
Recorded at WESTERN RECORDERS STUDIO 2,
Hollywood, CA (2/6/68) • RCA VICTOR STUDIOS,
Hollywood, CA (2/8/68)
Featuring/DAVY JONES: *lead vocals* • DON RANDI:
piano • MIKE DEASY, AL HENDRICKSON & GERRY
McGEE: *guitar* • MAX BENNETT: *bass* •
EARL PALMER: *drums, percussion* •
MARION "BUDDY" CHILDERS & JACK
SHELDON: *trumpet* • GEORGE
ROBERTS: *trombone* • JOHN
CAVE, DAVID DUKE & ARTHUR
MAEBE: *French horn* • MILT
HOLLAND & JERRY WILLIAMS:
percussion • SAMUEL FREED,
NATHAN KAPROFF, GEORGE KAST,
MARVIN LIMONICK, ALEX MURRAY
& ERNO NEUFELD: *violin* • MARIE
FERA, EDGAR LUSTGARTEN, JACQUELINE
LUSTGARTEN & FREDERICK SEYKORA: *cello* •
SHORTY ROGERS: *arrangement* • TERESA HELFER:
unknown
From the album *The Birds, The Bees & The Monkees*
(E) (4/22/68)

4. **AUNTIE'S MUNICIPAL COURT**
(Michael Nesmith/Keith Allison)
Produced by THE MONKEES
Engineered by HANK CICALO
Recorded at RCA VICTOR STUDIOS, Hollywood, CA
(1/6/68, 1/15/68 & 1/16/68)
Featuring/MICKY DOLENZ: *lead vocals* • MICHAEL
NESMITH: *harmony vocals, guitar* • KEITH
ALLISON & BILL CHADWICK: *guitar* • RICK DEY:
bass • EDDIE HOH: *drums* • HARRY NILSSON:
unknown
From the album *The Birds, The Bees & The Monkees*
(E) (4/22/68)

5. **P.O. BOX 9847**
(Tommy Boyce/Bobby Hart)
Produced by THE MONKEES
Engineered by HENRY LEWY
Recorded at UNITED RECORDERS STUDIO B,
Hollywood, CA (12/26/67) • UNITED
RECORDERS, Hollywood, CA (2/10/68)
Featuring/MICKY DOLENZ: *lead vocals* • GERRY
McGEE & LOUIE SHELTON: *guitar* • JOE
OSBORNE: *bass* • BILLY LEWIS: *drums* • VICTOR
ARNO & JACK PEPPER: *violin* • PHILIP
GOLDBERG: *viola* • RAY KELLEY: *cello* • DON
McGINNIS: *arrangement* • Unknown *keyboards
& backing vocals*
From the album *The Birds, The Bees & The Monkees*
(E) (4/22/68)

6. **ZOR AND ZAM**
(Bill Chadwick/John Chadwick)
Produced by THE MONKEES
Engineered by HANK CICALO

Recorded at RCA VICTOR STUDIOS, Hollywood, CA (1/7/68,
1/13/68, 1/18/68, 2/14/68, 2/17/68)
Featuring/MICKY DOLENZ: *lead vocals* • MIKE MELVOIN:
piano • KEITH ALLISON & BILL CHADWICK: *guitar* • MA
BENNETT, CHIP DOUGLAS & RICK DEY: *bass* • HA
BLAINE, EDDIE HOH, MILT HOLLAND & STAN LEVEY:
drums, percussion • MARION "BUDDY" CHILDERS, BOBB
HELFER, CLYDE REASINGER, JACK SHELDON & TON
TERRAN: *trumpet* • MILT BERNHART, RICHARD LEITH, LEW
McCREARY & FRANK ROSOLINO: *trombone* • JOH
LOWE: *sax* • NATHAN KAPROFF, GEORGE KAST, MARVI
LIMONICK, ALEX MURRAY, ERNO NEUFELD & AMBROS
RUSSO: *violin* • SHORTY ROGERS: *arrangement* •
HENRY DILTZ: *unknown*
From the album *The Birds, The Bees & The Monkees* **(E**
(4/22/68)

7. **CARLISLE WHEELING**
(First Recorded Version)
(Michael Nesmith)
Produced by THE MONKEES
Engineered by HANK CICALO
Recorded at RCA VICTOR STUDIOS, Hollywood, CA (11/4/67
Featuring/MICHAEL NESMITH: *lead vocals, guitar* • Othe
personnel unknown
Originally unissued • First collected on the album *Missin
Links* **(R)** (7/6/87)

8. **TEAR THE TOP RIGHT OFF MY HEAR**
(Peter Tork)
Produced by THE MONKEES
Engineer(s) unknown
Recorded at WESTERN RECORDERS, Hollywood, CA (2/5/68
2/6/68 & 2/8/68) • RCA VICTOR STUDIOS, Hollywood
CA (2/12/68)
Featuring/PETER TORK: *lead vocals, electric & fuzz guitar*
LANCE WAKELY: *acoustic guitar, harmonica* • RONAL
BROWN: *bass* • DEWEY MARTIN &/or BUDDY MILE
drums • MICKY DOLENZ: *backing vocals*
Originally unissued • First collected on the album *Listen 1
The Band* **(V)** (10/1/91)

9. **THE GIRL I LEFT BEHIND ME**
(First Recorded Version)
(Neil Sedaka/Carole Bayer)
Produced by THE MONKEES
Engineered by HANK CICALO
Recorded at RCA VICTOR STUDIOS, Hollywood, C
(10/31/67, 11/7/67 & 11/21/67)
Featuring/DAVY JONES: *lead vocals* • KEITH "RED" MITCHEL
piano • RED CALLENDER: *bass* • MILT HOLLAN
drums • VINCENT DeROSA: *French horn* • RICHAR
NOEL: *trombone* • JOHN GROSS: *sax* • ISRAEL BAKE
ROBERT BARENE & ELLIOTT FISHER: *violin* • FREDERIC
SEYKORA: *cello* • CHARLIE SMALLS: *arrangement*
EDDIE HOH & CHARLIE SMALLS: *unknown*
Originally unissued • First collected on the deluxe reissue
the album *The Birds, The Bees & The Monkees* (E–
(9/20/94)

10. **NINE TIMES BLUE**
(Michael Nesmith)
Produced by THE MONKEES
Engineered by PETER ABBOTT & PAT IERACI
Recorded at RCA VICTOR STUDIOS, Hollywood, CA (4/5/68
Featuring/MICHAEL NESMITH: *vocals, guitar* • RED RHODE
pedal steel guitar • CHIP DOUGLAS: *bass* • Unknow
additional guitar
Originally unissued • First collected on the album *Missin
Links* **(R)** (7/6/87)

11. **COME ON IN**
(Jo Mapes)
Produced by THE MONKEES
Engineer(s) unknown
Recorded at WESTERN RECORDERS, Hollywood, CA (2/8/6
2/9/68 & 2/11/68) • RCA VICTOR STUDIOS, Hollywoo
CA (2/12/68) • WESTERN RECORDERS STUDIO
Hollywood, CA (2/13/68)
Featuring/PETER TORK: *lead vocals, keyboards, guita
bass* • LANCE WAKELY: *guitar* • DEWEY MARTI
drums • BUDDY MILES: *unknown*
Originally unissued • First collected on the album *Missin
Links, Volume Two* **(U)** (1/23/90)

12. **D.W. WASHBURN**
(Jerry Leiber/Mike Stoller)
Produced by THE MONKEES
Engineered by HENRY LEWY (& others)
Recorded at RCA VICTOR STUDIOS, Hollywood, CA (2/17/
& 3/1/68)
Featuring/MICKY DOLENZ: *lead vocals* • MICHEL RUBI
tack piano • KEITH ALLISON: *electric guitar* • B

Disc 3

1968

CHADWICK: *acoustic guitar* • HENRY DILTZ: *banjo* • CHIP DOUGLAS: *bass* • JIM GORDON: *drums* • LARRY BUNKER: *glockenspiel* • BOBBY HELFER, CARROLL LEWIS & STU WILLIAMSON: *trumpet* • LOU BLACKBURN & HERBIE HARPER: *trombone* • BILL HOOD: *sax* • SHORTY ROGERS: *arrangement, conductor* • Unknown *backing vocals*
Originally issued as Colgems single #1023 (6/8/68); Pop #19 • First collected on the albums *Monkeemania: 40 Timeless Hits From The Monkees* **(N)** (10/79) & *Monkee Business* **(O)** (11/82)

3. **IT'S NICE TO BE WITH YOU**
(Jerry Goldstein)
Produced by THE MONKEES
Engineered by HENRY LEWY (& others)
Recorded at WESTERN RECORDERS STUDIO 2, Hollywood, CA (2/6/68) • RCA VICTOR STUDIOS, Hollywood, CA (2/7/68, 2/9/68 & 3/14/68)
Featuring/DAVY JONES: *lead vocals* • MIKE MELVOIN: *keyboards* • JAMES BURTON, MIKE DEASY, AL HENDRICKSON & GERRY McGEE: *guitar* • MAX BENNETT: *bass* • EARL PALMER: *drums, percussion* • MILT HOLLAND & JERRY WILLIAMS: *percussion* • MARION "BUDDY" CHILDERS, BOBBY HELFER, OLLIE MITCHELL & JACK SHELDON: *trumpet* • VINCENT DeROSA, DAVID DUKE, RICHARD PERISSI: *French horn* • LOU BLACKBURN & LEW McCREARY: *trombone* • MARTY BERMAN & BILL HOOD: *sax* • SAMUEL FREED, NATHAN KAPROFF, GEORGE KAST, MARVIN LIMONICK, ALEX MURRAY & ERNO NEUFELD: *violin* • MARIE FERA, JACQUELINE LUSTGARTEN, KURT REHER & ELEANOR SLATKIN: *cello* • SHORTY ROGERS: *arrangement, conductor*
Originally issued as Colgems single #1023 (6/8/68); Pop #51 • First collected on the album *The Monkees* **(M)** (7/76)

ST. MATTHEW
(Michael Nesmith)
Produced by MICHAEL NESMITH & FELTON JARVIS
Engineered by AL PACHUCKI (& others)
Recorded at unknown studio, Nashville, TN (6/2/68) • WALLY HEIDER RECORDING STUDIO 3, Hollywood, CA (6/12/68)
Featuring/MICHAEL NESMITH: *lead vocals* • DAVID BRIGGS: *piano* • WAYNE MOSS: *electric guitar* • HAROLD BRADLEY: *guitar* • LLOYD GREEN: *pedal steel guitar* • BOBBY THOMPSON: *banjo* • BUDDY SPICHER: *fiddle* • NORBERT PUTNAM: *bass* • JERRY CARRIGAN: *drums* • CHARLIE McCOY: *harmonica* • Unknown *Hammond organ, cowbell, tambourine & maracas*
Originally unissued • First collected on the album *Missing Links, Volume Two* **(U)** (1/23/90)

PORPOISE SONG (Theme From Head)
(Single Version)
(Gerry Goffin/Carole King)
Produced by GERRY GOFFIN
Engineered by CHRIS HINSHAW (& others)
Recorded at CALIFORNIA RECORDERS, Hollywood, CA (2/26/68 & 2/28/68) • WALLY HEIDER RECORDING, Hollywood, CA (2/29/68) • AMIGO RECORDING STUDIO, North Hollywood, CA (8/4/68 & 8/5/68) • Unknown studio (10/31/68)
Featuring/MICKY DOLENZ: *lead vocals* • LEON RUSSELL & RALPH SCHUCKETT: *keyboards* • KEN BLOOM & DANNY KORTCHMAR: *guitar* • DOUG LUBAHN: *bass* • MICHAEL NEY: *drums* • JOHN HOENIG: *percussion* • WILLIAM HINSHAW & JULES JACOB: *horns* • GREGORY BEMKO, DAVID FILERMAN, JAN KELLEY & JACQUELINE LUSTGARTEN: *cello* • MAX BENNETT, CLYDE "WHITEY" HOGGAN, JIM HUGHART & JERRY SCHEFF: *string bass* • DAVY JONES: *backing vocals* • RUSS TITELMAN: *conductor* • JACK NITZSCHE: *arrangement*
Originally issued as Colgems single #1031 (10/5/68); Pop #62 • First collected on the albums *Monkeemania: 40 Timeless Hits From The Monkees* **(N)** (10/79) & *Monkee Business* **(O)** (11/82) • An edited version was included on the album *Head* **(F)** (12/1/68)

AS WE GO ALONG
(Carole King/Toni Stern)
Produced by THE MONKEES
Engineer(s) unknown
Recorded at WALLY HEIDER'S, Hollywood, CA (5/30/68) •

UNITED RECORDERS STUDIO A, Hollywood, CA (7/31/68) • ORIGINAL SOUND, Hollywood, CA (8/1/68)
Featuring/MICKY DOLENZ: *lead vocals* • KEN BLOOM, RY COODER, CAROLE KING, DANNY KORTCHMAR, TONY McCASHEN & NEIL YOUNG: *guitar* • HARVEY NEWMARK: *bass* • EARL PALMER: *drums* • DENNY BRUCE & JOHN HOENIG: *percussion* • RUSS TITELMAN: *conductor* • JACK NITZSCHE: *arrangement* • Unknown *organ & flute*
Originally issued as Colgems single #1031 (10/5/68); Pop #106 • Also included on the album *Head* **(F)** (12/1/68)

17. **DITTY DIEGO—WAR CHANT**
(Jack Nicholson/Robert Rafelson)
Produced by THE MONKEES
Engineer(s) unknown
Recorded at RCA VICTOR STUDIOS, Hollywood, CA (8/3/68)
Featuring/MICKY DOLENZ, DAVY JONES, MICHAEL NESMITH & PETER TORK: *vocals* • MICHEL RUBINI: *piano*
From the album *Head* **(F)** (12/1/68)

18. **CIRCLE SKY (Live)**
(Michael Nesmith)
Produced by THE MONKEES
Engineer(s) unknown
Recorded at VALLEY AUDITORIUM, Salt Lake City, UT (5/17/68) • RCA VICTOR STUDIOS, Hollywood, CA (5/21/68)
Featuring/MICHAEL NESMITH: *lead vocals, guitar* • DAVY JONES: *organ, percussion* • PETER TORK: *bass* • MICKY DOLENZ: *drums*
Originally unissued • First collected on the albums *Monkeemania: 40 Timeless Hits From The Monkees* **(N)** (10/79) & *Missing Links, Volume Two* **(U)** (1/23/90)

19. **CAN YOU DIG IT**
(Peter Tork)
Produced by THE MONKEES
Engineer(s) unknown
Recorded at WESTERN RECORDERS, Hollywood, CA (1/28/68, 2/1/68 & 2/3/68) • RCA VICTOR STUDIOS, Hollywood, CA (1/29/68, 1/30/68, 1/31/68 & 3/8/68)
Featuring/MICKY DOLENZ: *lead vocals* • PETER TORK: *electric guitar, bass* • LANCE WAKELY: *acoustic guitar* • DEWEY MARTIN: *drums* • CHESTER ANDERSON, DOMINICK DeMIERI, MICHAEL GLASS, EDDIE HOH & BUDDY MILES: *unknown*
From the album *Head* **(F)** (12/1/68)

20. **DADDY'S SONG**
(Previously Unissued Long Version)
(Harry Nilsson)
Produced by THE MONKEES
Engineered by HANK CICALO, PETER ABBOTT, HENRY LEWY (& others)
Recorded at RCA VICTOR STUDIOS, Hollywood, CA (1/10/68, 1/16/68, 1/19/68, 3/1/68, 3/23/68 & 3/29/68) • SUNSET SOUND RECORDERS, Hollywood, CA (4/4/68)
Featuring/DAVY JONES: *lead vocals* • MICHEL RUBINI: *piano* • KEITH ALLISON, BILL CHADWICK & MICHAEL NESMITH: *guitar* • RICK DEY: *bass* • EDDIE HOH: *drums* • PETE CANDOLI, MARION "BUDDY" CHILDERS, BOBBY HELFER & TONY TERRAN: *trumpet* • RICHARD LEITH & LEW McCREARY: *trombone* • JUSTIN DiTULLIO, RAPHAEL KRAMER, EMMET SARGEANT & ELEANOR SLATKIN: *cello* • SHORTY ROGERS: *arrangement*
From the album *Head* **(F)** (12/1/68)

21. **LONG TITLE: DO I HAVE TO DO THIS ALL OVER AGAIN**
(Peter Tork)
Produced by THE MONKEES
Engineer(s) unknown
Recorded at SUNSET SOUND RECORDERS, Hollywood, CA (1/25/68 & 1/26/68) • RCA VICTOR STUDIOS, Hollywood, CA (1/27/68 & 2/12/68) • WESTERN RECORDERS, Hollywood, CA (1/28/68, 2/1/68, 2/3/68, 2/4/68, 2/5/68, 2/10/68 & 2/14/68)
Featuring/PETER TORK: *lead vocals, guitar, bass* • LANCE WAKELY: *electric guitar* • DEWEY MARTIN &/or BUDDY MILES: *drums* • DAVY JONES: *backing vocals*
From the album *Head* **(F)** (12/1/68)

1. **TEAR DROP CITY**
(Tommy Boyce/Bobby Hart)
Produced by TOMMY BOYCE & BOBBY HART
Engineered by DAVID HASSINGER
Recorded at RCA VICTOR STUDIO B, Hollywood, CA
(10/26/66, 10/30/66, 10/31/66 & 11/6/66)
Featuring/MICKY DOLENZ: *lead vocals* • BOBBY HART:
organ • WAYNE ERWIN: *guitar, backing vocals* •
GERRY McGEE & LOUIE SHELTON: *guitar* • LARRY
TAYLOR: *bass* • BILLY LEWIS: *drums* • GENE ESTES:
percussion • TOMMY BOYCE & BOBBY HART: *back-
ing vocals, arrangement* • RON HICKLIN: *backing
vocals*
Originally issued as Colgems single #5000 (2/8/69);
Pop #56 • Also included on the album *Instant
Replay* (G) (2/15/69)

2. **A MAN WITHOUT A DREAM**
(Gerry Goffin/Carole King)
Produced by BONES HOWE
Engineered by BONES HOWE
Recorded at WALLY HEIDER RECORDING STUDIO 3,
Hollywood, CA (11/7/68) • WESTERN RECORDERS,
Hollywood, CA (1/10/69 & 1/11/69)
Featuring/DAVY JONES: *lead vocals* • LARRY KNECHTEL &
JIMMY ROWLES: *keyboards* • DON ADDRISI, MIKE
DEASY & TOMMY TEDESCO: *guitar* • JOE STEPANSKY:
bass • HAL BLAINE: *drums* • CONTE CANDOLI,
MARION "BUDDY" CHILDERS & LLOYD LUHMAN:
trumpet • BOB EDMONDSON & LEW McCREARY:
trombone • JAMES DECKER, VINCENT DeROSA,
WILLIAM HINSHAW & RICHARD PERISSI: *French horn* •
BOB ALCIVAR, BILL HOLMAN & BONES HOWE:
arrangement
Originally issued as Colgems single #5000 (2/8/69) • Also
included on the album *Instant Replay* (G)
(2/15/69)

3. **THROUGH THE LOOKING GLASS**
(Tommy Boyce/Bobby Hart/Red Baldwin)
Produced by TOMMY BOYCE & BOBBY HART
Engineered by HENRY LEWY
Recorded at UNITED RECORDERS
STUDIO B, Hollywood, CA (12/30/67) •
UNITED RECORDERS, Hollywood, CA
(12/20/68)
Featuring/MICKY DOLENZ: *lead
vocals* • BOBBY HART: *tack piano* •
KEITH ALLISON, GERRY McGEE
& LOUIE SHELTON: *guitar* • JOE
OSBORNE: *bass* • BILLY LEWIS:
drums • ALAN ESTES: *percussion* •
DON McGINNIS: *arrangement* •
Unknown *horns & strings*
From the album *Instant Replay* (G) (2/15/69)

4. **I WON'T BE THE SAME WITHOUT HER**
(Gerry Goffin/Carole King)
Produced by MICHAEL NESMITH
Engineered by HANK CICALO & DAVID HASSINGER
Recorded at RCA VICTOR STUDIO A, Hollywood, CA
(7/18/66 & 7/30/66) • RCA VICTOR STUDIO B,
Hollywood, CA (8/30/66)
Featuring/MICHAEL NESMITH: *lead vocals* • JAMES
BURTON, GLEN CAMPBELL, AL CASEY & MIKE DEASY:
guitar • LARRY KNECHTEL & BOB WEST: *bass* • HAL
BLAINE & JIM GORDON: *drums* • GARY COLEMAN &
FRANK DeVITO: *percussion* • MICHAEL NESMITH:
arrangement • Unknown *Danelectro bass &
backing vocals*
From the album *Instant Replay* (G) (2/15/69)

5. **YOU AND I**
(Davy Jones/Bill Chadwick)
Produced by DAVY JONES
Engineered by HENRY LEWY
Recorded at WALLY HEIDER RECORDING STUDIO 3,
Hollywood, CA (5/10/68) • SUNSET SOUND
RECORDERS, Hollywood, CA (6/19/68 & 6/21/68) •
RCA VICTOR STUDIOS, Hollywood, CA (9/20/68)
Featuring/DAVY JONES: *lead vocals* • LARRY KNECHTEL:
organ • BILL CHADWICK, GERRY McGEE, LOUIE
SHELTON & NEIL YOUNG: *guitar* • JOE OSBORNE:
bass • HAL BLAINE: *drums* • SHORTY ROGERS:
arrangement • STEVE PITTS: *unknown*
From the album *Instant Replay* (G) (2/15/69)

6. **WHILE I CRY**
(Michael Nesmith)
Produced by MICHAEL NESMITH
Engineered by HANK CICALO
Recorded at RCA VICTOR STUDIO, Hollywood, CA (1/14/68
& 1/15/68)
Featuring/MICHAEL NESMITH: *lead vocals, guitar* • KEITH
ALLISON & BILL CHADWICK: *guitar* • RICK DEY:

Disc 4
1969-96

bass • EDDIE HOH: *drums* • MICHAEL NESMI
arrangement • HARRY NILSSON: *unknown*
From the album *Instant Replay* (G) (2/15/69)

7. **SHORTY BLACKWELL**
(Micky Dolenz)
Produced by MICKY DOLENZ
Engineered by HENRY LEWY & HANK CICALO
Recorded at RCA VICTOR STUDIOS, Hollywood,
(1/19/68 & 2/15/68) • UNITED RECORDE
Hollywood, CA (2/4/68) • WESTERN RECORD
STUDIO 1, Hollywood, CA (4/9/68) • WESTE
RECORDERS, Hollywood, CA (4/30/68, 5/2/68
6/7/68)
Featuring/MICKY DOLENZ: *lead vocals* • BILL CHADW
& TOMMY TEDESCO: *guitar* • MICHEL RUB
piano • MAX BENNETT: *bass* • JIM GORDO
drums • VICTOR FELDMAN, JOE PORCARO & E
RICHARDS: *percussion* • BUD BRISBOIS, MARI
"BUDDY" CHILDERS, BOBBY HELFER, OLLIE MITCH
& RAY TRISCARI: *trumpet* • GEORGE ROBERTS
KENNY SHROYER: *trombone* • VINCENT DeRO
DAVID DUKE & RICHARD PERISSI: *French hor*
RONALD LANGINGER, TED NASH & CLIFFO
SHANK: *flute* • GEORGE BERRES, ANATOL KAMINS
BERNARD KUNDELL, ERNO NEUFELD, NATHAN R
& JOE STEPANSKY: *violin* • JUSTIN DiTUL
ARMAND KAPROFF & EDGAR LUSTGARTEN: *cell
COCO DOLENZ: *backing vocals* • SHO
ROGERS: *arrangement*
From the album *Instant Replay* (G) (2/15/69)

8. **IF I EVER GET TO SAGINAW AGAI**
(Jack Keller/Bob Russell)
Produced by THE MONKEES
Engineer(s) unknown
Recorded at RCA VICTOR STUDIOS, Hollywood,
(3/9/68) • RCA VICTOR STUDIO C, Hollywood,
(1/31/69) • UNITED RECORDERS, Hollywood,
(3/6/69)
Featuring/MICHAEL NESMITH: *lead vocals* • M
MELVOIN: *piano* • DENNIS BUDIMIR, AL CASEY, M
DEASY, DEL KACHER & LOUIE SHELTON: *guitar* • M
BENNETT: *bass* • EARL PALMER: *drums* • M
HOLLAND & STAN LEVEY: *percussion* • J
GOOTKIN, ROBERT JUNG, GEORGE POO
HEIMANN WEINSTEIN & WILLIAM WEISS: *violi*
GARETH NUTTYCOMBE: *viola* • DOUGLAS DA
cello • DON McGINNIS: *string arrangemer*
SHORTY ROGERS: *arrangement* • BOBBY HEL
unknown
Originally unissued • First collected on the alb
Missing Links, Volume Two (U) (1/23/90)

9. **SMILE**
(Davy Jones)
Produced by DAVY JONES
Engineered by HENRY LEWY
Recorded at WALLY HEIDER RECORDING, Hollywood
(5/10/68)
Featuring/DAVY JONES: *lead vocals* • LARRY KNECH
keyboards • BILL CHADWICK, GERRY McGEE &
YOUNG: *guitar* • JOE OSBORNE: *bass* •
BLAINE: *drums* • SHORTY ROGERS: *arrangeme*
STEVE PITTS: *unknown* • Unknown *backing vo*
Originally unissued • First collected on the de
reissue of the album *Instant Replay* (C
(1/24/95)

10. **LISTEN TO THE BAND** (Single Versio
(Michael Nesmith)
Produced by MICHAEL NESMITH
Engineered by AL PACHUCKI (& others)
Recorded at RCA VICTOR STUDIOS, Nashville,
(6/1/68) • RCA VICTOR STUDIOS, Hollywood
(12/9/68) • GOLD STAR RECORDING STU
Hollywood, CA (12/68)
Featuring/MICHAEL NESMITH: *lead vocals, guit*
DAVID BRIGGS: *piano* • MICHEL RUBINI: *org*
WAYNE MOSS: *electric guitar* • HAROLD BRADL
BILLY SANFORD: *guitar* • LLOYD GREEN: *pedal*
guitar • BOBBY THOMPSON: *banjo* • BU
SPICHER: *fiddle* • NORBERT PUTNAM: *bass* • J
CARRIGAN: *drums* • BUD BRISBOIS, MAR
"BUDDY" CHILDERS & RAY TRISCARI: *trumpet* • L
NASH: *trombone* • JOHN KITZMILLER: *tuba* •
McGINNIS & MICHAEL SALUZZI: *horns* • SHO
ROGERS: *horn arrangement* • MICHAEL NESI
arrangement • Unknown *bass harmon
cowbell, tambourine & maracas*
Originally issued as Colgems single #5004 (4/26
Pop #63 • First collected on the album *Liste
The Band* (V) (10/1/91) • An extended ve
was included on the album *The Mon
Present*

92

SOMEDAY MAN
(Roger Nichols/Paul Williams)
Produced by BONES HOWE
Engineered by BONES HOWE
Recorded at WALLY HEIDER RECORDING STUDIO 3, Hollywood, CA (11/7/68 & 1/4/69) • WESTERN RECORDERS, Hollywood, CA (1/10/69 & 1/11/69)
Featuring/DAVY JONES: *lead vocals* • LARRY KNECHTEL & JIMMY ROWLES: *keyboards* • DON ADDRISI, MIKE DEASY & TOMMY TEDESCO: *guitar* • JOE OSBORNE: *bass* • HAL BLAINE: *drums* • CONTE CANDOLI, MARION "BUDDY" CHILDERS & LLOYD LUHMAN: *trumpet* • BOB EDMONDSON & LEW McCREARY: *trombone* • JAMES DECKER, VINCENT DeROSA, WILLIAM HINSHAW & RICHARD PERISSI: *French horn* • BOB ALCIVAR, BILL HOLMAN & BONES HOWE: *arrangement* • Unknown *percussion & handclaps*
Originally issued as Colgems single #5004 (4/26/69); *Pop #81* • First collected on the album **The Monkees (M)** (7/76)

SOME OF SHELLY'S BLUES
(Michael Nesmith)
Produced by MICHAEL NESMITH & FELTON JARVIS
Engineered by BILL VANDEVORT
Recorded at RCA VICTOR STUDIOS, Nashville, TN (5/29/68)
Featuring/MICHAEL NESMITH: *vocals* • LARRY BUTLER: *piano* • BILLY SANFORD: *electric guitar* • LLOYD GREEN: *pedal steel guitar* • SONNY OSBORNE: *banjo* • BOBBY DYSON: *bass* • WILLIAM ACKERMAN: *drums* • Unknown *harmonica*
Originally unissued • First collected on the album **Missing Links, Volume Two (U)** (1/23/90)

MOMMY AND DADDY
(Micky Dolenz)
Produced by MICKY DOLENZ
Engineer(s) unknown
Recorded at RCA VICTOR STUDIOS, Hollywood, CA (8/1/68 & 12/9/68)
Featuring/MICKY DOLENZ: *lead vocals* • MICHEL RUBINI: *piano* • BUD BRISBOIS, MARION "BUDDY" CHILDERS & RAY TRISCARI: *trumpet* • DICK NASH • JOHN KITZMILLER: *tuba* • DON McGINNIS & MICHAEL SALUZZI: *horns* • MICKY DOLENZ & SHORTY ROGERS: *arrangement* • PAT COGHLAN & DON DEMIERI: *unknown* • Unknown *guitar, bass & drums*
Originally issued as Colgems single #5005 (9/6/69); *Pop #109* • Also included on the album **The Monkees Present (I)** (10/69)

GOOD CLEAN FUN
(Michael Nesmith)
Produced by MICHAEL NESMITH
Engineered by AL PACHUCKI
Recorded at RCA VICTOR STUDIOS, Nashville, TN (6/1/68)
Featuring/MICHAEL NESMITH: *lead vocals* • DAVID BRIGGS: *piano* • WAYNE MOSS: *electric guitar* • HAROLD BRADLEY & BILLY SANFORD: *guitar* • LLOYD GREEN: *pedal steel guitar* • BOBBY THOMPSON: *banjo* • BUDDY SPICHER: *fiddle* • NORBERT PUTNAM: *bass* • JERRY CARRIGAN: *drums* • MICHAEL NESMITH: *arrangement* • Unknown *jawbone & wood block*
Originally issued as Colgems single #5005 (9/6/69); *Pop #82* • Also included on the album **The Monkees Present (I)** (10/69)

LOOKING FOR THE GOOD TIMES
(Tommy Boyce/Bobby Hart)
Produced by TOMMY BOYCE & BOBBY HART
Engineered by DAVID HASSINGER
Recorded at RCA VICTOR STUDIO B, Hollywood, CA (10/26/66,10/30/66, 11/6/66 & 11/12/66)
Featuring/DAVY JONES: *lead vocals* • BOBBY HART: *organ, backing vocals* • WAYNE ERWIN, GERRY McGEE & LOUIE SHELTON: *guitar* • LARRY TAYLOR: *bass* • BILLY LEWIS: *drums* • GENE ESTES: *percussion* • TOMMY BOYCE, MICKY DOLENZ & RON HICKLIN: *backing vocals*
From the album **The Monkees Present (I)** (10/69)

STEAM ENGINE
(Chip Douglas)
Produced by CHIP DOUGLAS
Engineered by EDDIE BRACKETT (& others)
Recorded at WESTERN RECORDERS STUDIO 1, Hollywood, CA (5/12/69) • RCA VICTOR STUDIOS, Hollywood, CA (7/8/69)
Featuring/MICKY DOLENZ: *lead vocals* • LARRY KNECHTEL: *keyboards* • CLARENCE WHITE: *guitar* • RED RHODES: *pedal steel guitar* • LYLE RITZ: *bass* • JIM GORDON & EDDIE HOH: *drums* • GARY COLEMAN: *percussion* • RAY BROWN, BILL PETERSON, SANFORD SKINNER & TONY TERRAN: *trumpet* • BOBBY KNIGHT & LEW McCREARY: *trombone* • BILL GREEN, BOB HARDAWAY & SID

MILLER: *sax* • JERRY YESTER: *arrangement* • Unknown *backing vocals*
Originally unissued • First collected on the albums *Monkeemania: 40 Timeless Hits From The Monkees* **(N)** (10/79) & *Monkee Business* **(O)** (11/82)

17. **I NEVER THOUGHT IT PECULIAR**
(Tommy Boyce/Bobby Hart)
Produced by TOMMY BOYCE & BOBBY HART
Engineer(s) unknown
Recorded at RCA VICTOR STUDIO B, Hollywood, CA (10/28/66) • THE SOUND FACTORY, Hollywood, CA (9/5/69 & 9/12/69)
Featuring/DAVY JONES: *lead vocals* • GERRY McGEE, WAYNE ERWIN & LOUIE SHELTON: *guitar* • LARRY TAYLOR: *bass* • BILLY LEWIS: *drums* • GENE ESTES: *percussion* • CHUCK FINDLEY: *trumpet* • DICK HYDE: *trombone* • ALAN ROBINSON: *French horn* • JAY MIGLIORI: *sax* • HAROLD AYRES, JOHN DeVOOGDT, JAMES GETZOFF, WILLIAM HYMANSON & NORMAN SERKIN: *violin* • GARETH NUTTYCOME: *viola* • FREDERICK SEYKORA: *cello* • JIMMIE HASKELL: *arrangement* • MIKE ANTHONY & JOY LULE: *unknown* • TOMMY BOYCE, BOBBY HART & RON HICKLIN: *backing vocals*
From the album **Changes (J)** (6/70)

18. **MIDNIGHT TRAIN**
(Micky Dolenz)
Produced by MICKY DOLENZ
Engineered by PETER ABBOTT (& others)
Recorded at RCA VICTOR STUDIOS, Hollywood, CA (7/16/69)
Featuring/MICKY DOLENZ: *lead vocals* • JAMES BURTON & LOUIE SHELTON: *guitar* • JOE OSBORNE: *bass* • HAL BLAINE: *drums* • TOMMY MORGAN: *harmonica* • COCO DOLENZ: *backing vocals* • Unknown *banjo*
From the album **Changes (J)** (6/70)

19. **OH MY MY**
(Jeff Barry/Andy Kim)
Produced by JEFF BARRY
Engineered by MIKE MORAN
Recorded at unknown studio, New York, NY (2/5/70)
Featuring/MICKY DOLENZ: *lead vocals* • Other personnel unknown
Originally issued as Colgems single #5011 (4/70); *#98* • Also included on the album **Changes (J)** (6/70)

20. **I LOVE YOU BETTER**
(Jeff Barry/Andy Kim)
Produced by JEFF BARRY
Engineered by MIKE MORAN
Recorded at unknown studio, New York, NY (2/5/70)
Featuring/MICKY DOLENZ: *lead vocals* • Other personnel unknown
Originally issued as Colgems single #5011 (4/70) • Also included on the album **Changes (J)** (6/70)

21. **DO YOU FEEL IT TOO?**
(Jeff Barry/Andy Kim)
Produced by JEFF BARRY
Engineered by MIKE MORAN
Recorded at unknown studio, New York, NY (3/26/70)
Featuring/DAVY JONES: *lead vocals* • Other personnel unknown
From the album **Changes (J)** (6/70)

22. **DO IT IN THE NAME OF LOVE –**
Micky Dolenz & Davy Jones
(Bobby Bloom/Neil Goldberg)
Produced by JEFF BARRY
Engineer(s) unknown
Recorded at unknown studio, New York, NY (9/22/70)
Featuring/MICKY DOLENZ & DAVY JONES: *lead vocals* • Other personnel unknown
Originally issued as Bell single #986 (4/71) • First collected on the deluxe reissue of the album **Changes (J-3)** (9/20/94)

23. **THAT WAS THEN, THIS IS NOW –**
Micky Dolenz & Peter Tork
(Vance Brescia)
Produced by MICHAEL LLOYD
Engineer(s) unknown
Recorded at HEAVEN STUDIOS, Beverly Hills, CA (5/30/86)
Featuring/MICKY DOLENZ: *lead vocals* • JIM COX: *piano* • MICHAEL LLOYD: *synthesizer, backing*

vocals • LAURENCE JUBER: *electric guitar* • DEN▓
BELFIELD & DEAN PARKS: *bass* • PAUL LEIM: *drums* • PE▓
TORK: *backing vocals*
Originally issued as Arista single #ASI-9505 (6/27/86); Pop #2▓
Also included on the album ***Then & Now...The Best O***
***The Monkees* (P)** (6/86)

24. HEART AND SOUL
(Andrew Howell/Simon Byrne)
Produced by ROGER BECHIRIAN
Engineered by ROBERT SALCEDO & ROGER BECHIRIAN, with C▓
KANE & SCOTT GORDON
Recorded at CHEROKEE RECORDING STUDIOS, Hollywood,
(5/22/87, 6/11/87 & 7/2/87)
Featuring/MICKY DOLENZ: *lead vocals* • MICHAEL EG▓
keyboards, programming • MARK CHRISTIAN: *guita*
GEORGE HAWKINS: *bass* • CURLY SMITH: *drums* • RO▓
BECHIRIAN: *percussion, arrangement* • CRAIG OST▓
percussion • MATT HARRIS: *backing vocals*
Originally issued as Rhino single #RNOR-74408 (7/87); Pop #5▓
Also included on the album ***Pool It!* (S)** (8/1/87)

25. MGBGT (Live)
(Peter Tork)
Produced by DAVY JONES, MICKY DOLENZ & PETER TORK
Engineered by JAY MESSINA
Recorded live on tour (1986) • Mixed at THE RECORD PLA▓
New York, NY
Featuring/PETER TORK: *lead vocals, guitar* • LARRY NELS▓
keyboards • DUSTY HANVEY: *guitar* • MARK CLA▓
bass • EDDIE ZYNE: *drums* • JIM O'CONNOR & ▓
SEAMAN: *trumpet* • KEVIN OSBORNE: *trombone* • J▓
LESLIE: *sax* • MICKY DOLENZ & DAVY JONES: *bac*▓
vocals
From the album ***20th Anniversary Tour 1986* (T)** (7/87) • ▓
issued as Rhino single #RNOR-74408 (7/87)

26. EVERY STEP OF THE WAY (Single Versio▓
(Ian Hunter/Mark Clarke)
Produced by ROGER BECHIRIAN
Engineered by ROBERT SALCEDO & ROGER BECHIRIAN, with C▓
KANE & SCOTT GORDON • Remixed by DAVY JON▓
MARK CLARKE
Recorded at CHEROKEE RECORDING STUDIOS, Hollywood, C▓
Featuring/DAVY JONES: *lead vocals* • MICHAEL E▓
keyboards, programming, backing vocals • M▓
CHRISTIAN & LOU NAKTIN: *guitar* • DAVEY FARAG▓
bass • CURLY SMITH: *drums* • ROGER BECHIR▓
percussion, arrangement • CRAIG OSTBO: *percussi*▓
JIM THOMPSON: *sax* • MATT HARRIS: *backing vocals*
Originally issued as Rhino single #RNOR-74410 (11/87) • ▓
collected on the album ***Listen To The Band***
(10/1/91) • An alternate mix was included on the alb▓
***Pool It!* (S)** (8/1/87)

27. OH, WHAT A NIGHT
(Davy Jones)
Produced by THE MONKEES
Engineered by MIKE McDONALD & BOB BULLOCK, with S▓
MIXDORF, TERRY BATES, GRANT GREEN & TIM GERRON
Recorded at NRG RECORDING SERVICES, North Hollywood, ▓
SOUND STAGE STUDIO, Nashville, TN • Mixed at WEST▓
AUDIO, Los Angeles, CA (6/96-8/96)
Featuring/DAVY JONES: *lead vocals, percussion* • PETER T▓
keyboards, bass, backing vocals • MICHAEL NESM▓
guitar, backing vocals • MICKY DOLENZ: *drums, bac*▓
vocals
From the album ***Justus* (Y)** (10/15/96)

28. YOU AND I
(Micky Dolenz/Davy Jones)
Produced by THE MONKEES
Engineered by MIKE McDONALD & BOB BULLOCK, with S▓
MIXDORF, TERRY BATES, GRANT GREEN & TIM GERRON
Recorded at NRG RECORDING SERVICES, North Hollywood, ▓
SOUND STAGE STUDIO, Nashville, TN • Mixed at WEST▓
AUDIO, Los Angeles, CA (6/96-8/96)
Featuring/DAVY JONES: *lead vocals, guitar, percussion* • M▓
DOLENZ: *harmony vocals, drums* • MICHAEL NESM▓
electric guitar, backing vocals • PETER TORK: *b*▓
backing vocals
From the album ***Justus* (Y)** (10/15/96)

NOTE: Numbers in italics (following original single rel▓
information) denote peak positions obtained on *Billbo*▓
"Hot 100" chart — courtesy BPI Communications and ▓
Whitburn's Record Research Publications. Code lette▓
brackets (following original album release information) re▓
the listings in the following discography & the correspo▓
minis.

Monkees

RE OF THE

Of The Monkees

quarters

Aquarius,
corn & Jones Ltd.

ds, The Bees
Monkees

HEAD

MONKEES
STANT REPLAY

Replay

H. The Monkees Greatest Hits

I. The Monkees Present

J. Changes

K. Barrel Full Of Monkees

L. The Monkees Greatest Hits

M. The Monkees

Select Album Discography:

I. THE ORIGINAL COLGEMS RELEASES (& REISSUES)

The Monkees
Produced by TOMMY BOYCE, BOBBY HART, JACK KELLER & MICHAEL NESMITH
Music Supervision: DON KIRSHNER
Music Coordinators: LESTER SILL & EMIL LaVIOLA
(A) Colgems #COS-101 (10/66); *LPs #1*
(A-2) Rhino #RNLP-70140 (6/86); *LPs #92*
(A-3) Rhino #R2-71790 (9/20/94)

More Of The Monkees
Produced by TOMMY BOYCE, BOBBY HART, NEIL SEDAKA, CAROLE BAYER, MICHAEL NESMITH, JEFF BARRY, JACK KELLER, GERRY GOFFIN & CAROLE KING
Music Supervision: DON KIRSHNER
Music Coordinators: LESTER SILL & EMIL LaVIOLA
(B) Colgems #COS-102 (1/10/67); *LPs #1*
(B-2) Rhino #RNLP-70142 (5/86); *LPs #96*
(B-3) Rhino #R2-71791 (11/15/94)

Headquarters
Produced by DOUGLAS FARTHING HATLELID
(C) Colgems #COS-103 (5/22/67); *LPs #1*
(C-2) Rhino #RNLP-70143 (5/86); *LPs #121*
(C-3) Rhino #R2-71792 (1/24/95)

Pisces, Aquarius, Capricorn & Jones Ltd.
Produced by CHIP DOUGLAS
Music Supervision: LESTER SILL
(D) Colgems #COS-104 (11/14/67); *LPs #1*
(D-2) Rhino #RNLP-70141 (6/86); *LPs #124*
(D-3) Rhino #R2-71793 (1/24/95)

The Birds, The Bees & The Monkees
Produced by THE MONKEES & CHIP DOUGLAS
Music Supervision: LESTER SILL
(E) Colgems #COS-109 (4/22/68); *LPs #3*
(E-2) Rhino #RNLP-144 (1985); *LPs #145*
(E-3) Rhino #R2-71794 (9/20/94)

Head
Produced by THE MONKEES & GERRY GOFFIN
Incidental Music Composed & Conducted by KEN THORNE
Original Album Coordinator: JACK NICHOLSON
(F) Colgems #COS-5008 (12/1/68); *LPs #45*
(F-2) Rhino #RNLP-145 (1985)
(F-3) Rhino #R2-71795 (11/15/94)

Instant Replay
Produced by TOMMY BOYCE, BOBBY HART, MICHAEL NESMITH, MICKY DOLENZ, DAVY JONES, CAROLE BAYER, NEIL SEDAKA & BONES HOWE
Musical Coordinator: BRENDAN CAHILL
(G) Colgems #COS-113 (2/15/69); *LPs #32*
(G-2) Rhino #RNLP-146 (1985)
(G-3) Rhino #R2-71796 (1/24/95)

The Monkees Greatest Hits
Produced by CHIP DOUGLAS, THE MONKEES, JEFF BARRY, TOMMY BOYCE, BOBBY HART & MICHAEL NESMITH
(H) Colgems #COS-115 (6/69); *LPs #89*

The Monkees Present
Produced by MICKY DOLENZ, MICHAEL NESMITH, DAVID JONES, BILL CHADWICK, TOMMY BOYCE & BOBBY HART
Music Coordinator: BRENDAN CAHILL
(I) Colgems #COS-117 (10/11/69); *LPs #100*
(I-2) Rhino #RNLP-147 (1985)
(I-3) Rhino #R2-71797 (11/15/94)

Changes
Produced by JEFF BARRY, MICKY DOLENZ, TOMMY
      BOYCE & BOBBY HART
Previously Unissued Bonus Material (on J-3) Produced
      by BILL CHADWICK & DAVY JONES
Music Coordinator: BRENDAN CAHILL
(J) Colgems #COS-119 (6/70); *LPs #152*
(J-2) Rhino #RNLP-70148 (9/86); *LPs #152*
(J-3) Rhino #R2-71798 (9/20/94)

Barrel Full Of Monkees
Various Producers
(K) Colgems/RCA #SCOS-1001 (1/71)

II: SELECT POST-COLGEMS COLLECTIONS & REUNIONS

The Monkees Greatest Hits
Various Producers
(L) Arista #AL-4089 (7/76); *LPs #58*

The Monkees
Various Producers
(M) Laurie House/RCA #LH-8009 (7/76)

Monkeemania: 40 Timeless Hits From The Monkees
Various Producers
(N) Arista/EMI (AUST) #MONK-1/2 (10/79)

Monkee Business
Various Producers
(O) Rhino #RNLP-701 (11/82)

Then & Now...The Best Of The Monkees
Various Producers
(P) Arista #AL9-8432 (6/86); *LPs #21*

Live 1967
Produced by BURT SCHNEIDER & BOB RAFELSON
(Q) Rhino #RNLP-70139 (7/6/87)

Missing Links
Various Producers
(R) Rhino #RNLP-70150 (7/6/87)

Pool It!
Produced by ROGER BECHIRIAN
Musical Supervisor: LOU NAKTIN
(S) Rhino #RNIN/RNCD-70706 (8/1/87); *LPs #72*

20th Anniversary Tour 1986
Produced by DAVY JONES, MICKY DOLENZ &
      PETER TORK
(T) No label (limited release/sold at concerts)
      #FSH-71110 (7/87)

Missing Links, Volume Two
Various Producers
(U) Rhino #R2-70903 (1/23/90)

Listen To The Band
Various Producers
(V) Rhino #R2-70566 (10/1/91)

The Monkees Greatest Hits
Various Producers
(W) Rhino #R2-72190 (10/24/95)

Missing Links, Volume Three
Various Producers
(X) Rhino #R2-72153 (3/26/96)

Justus
Produced by THE MONKEES
(Y) Rhino #R2-72542 (10/15/96)

The Monkees Anthology
Various Producers
(Z) Rhino #R2-75269 (4/21/98)

NOTE: Numbers in italics (following album release information)
denote peak positions obtained on *Billboard*'s "Top LPs (&
Tapes)"/"Top Pop Albums" chart — courtesy BPI
Communications and Joel Whitburn's Record Research
Publications.

N. *Monkeemania: 40 Timeless Hits From The Monkees*

O. *Monkee Business*

P. *Then & Now...The Best Of The Monkees*

Q. *Live 1967*

R. *Missing Links*

S. *Pool It!*

T. *20th Anniversary Tour 1986*

U. *Missing Links, Volume Two*

V. *Listen To The Band*

W. *The Monkees Greatest Hits*

X. *Missing Links, Volume Three*

Y. *Justus*

Z. *The Monkees Anthol...*